Answers: P1 — P4

Section 1 — Numbers

Page 1 — Add, Subtract, Multiply and Divide

1   (18 − 6) ÷ (3 × 2) = 2 *[1 mark]*

2 a)   7 − (−6) = 7 + 6 = 13 °C *[1 mark]*

   b)   The difference between temperatures in London and Moscow is 7 − (−9) = 16 °C, so halfway will be 16 ÷ 2 = 8 °C away from both temperatures. −9 + 8 = −1 °C. *[1 mark]*

3
```
       2 1 0  remainder 7
   11 ⟌ 2 3¹1 7
```
There will be 210 staples in each stapler *[1 mark]* with 7 staples left over. *[1 mark]*

4 a)   3 sausage rolls: £1.10 × 3 = £3.30
         3 Cornish pasties: £2.05 × 3 = £6.15
         1 blueberry muffin: £0.90 × 1 = £0.90
         2 almond slices: £1.25 × 2 = £2.50

         £3.30
         £6.15
         £0.90
      + £2.50
         £12.85
           1 1

[2 marks available — 1 mark for multiplying the prices by the number of items correctly, 1 mark for the correct answer]

   b)
        1 9 9
      £2̸0̸.0̸0̸
     − £12.85
      £ 7.15 *[1 mark]*

Page 2 — Special Types of Number

1
⊗	2	3	✗	5	6	7	⑧	✗	10
11	12	13	14	15	✗	17	18	19	20
21	22	23	24	✗	26	㉗	28	29	30
31	32	33	34	35	✗	37	38	39	40

   a)   *[1 mark for crosses over the correct numbers]*

   b)   *[1 mark for circles over the correct numbers]*

2   Get rid of anything that doesn't end in 1, 3, 7 or 9:
9̵5̵ — ends in a 5 so is not prime

Now see if the remaining numbers divide by 3 or 7:
19 — doesn't divide by 3 or 7 so is prime.
1̵1̵1̵ — divides by 3 so is not prime.
2̵7̵ — divides by 3 so is not prime.
5̵7̵ — divides by 3 so is not prime.
4̵9̵ — divides by 7 so is not prime.
53 — doesn't divide by 3 or 7 so is prime.
3̵3̵ — divides by 3 so is not prime.
41 — doesn't divide by 3 or 7 so is prime.
2̵1̵ — divides by 3 and 7 so is not prime.
So the prime numbers are 19, 53 and 41.
[2 marks available — 2 marks for finding the three correct prime numbers, otherwise 1 mark for finding two correct primes or if a non-prime number is included as well as the three correct primes]

3 a) $6.543, \frac{5}{7}, \frac{763}{999}, \sqrt{9}, 99.9$ *[1 mark]*

   b) $\sqrt{2}, \pi$ *[1 mark]*

   c)   7 *[1 mark]*
       All the numbers in the box are real numbers.

Page 3

1 a)

| 8 cm | 3 cm | 24 cm² |
| 6 cm | 4 cm | 24 cm² |

[2 marks available — 2 marks for all rows correct, otherwise 1 mark for at least two rows correct]

   b)   1, 2, 3, 4, 6, 8, 12, 24 *[1 mark]*

2 a)   Multiples of 6:   6, 12, 18, 24, 30, 36, 42, 48, ...
       Multiples of 8:   8, 16, 24, 32, 40, 48, ...
       The Lotto numbers in both lists are 24 and 48. *[1 mark]*

   b)   Multiples of 8:   8, 16, 24, 32, 40, 48, ...
       Factors of 64:   1, 2, 4, 8, 16, 32, 64
       The Lotto number in both lists is 16. *[1 mark]*

3 a)

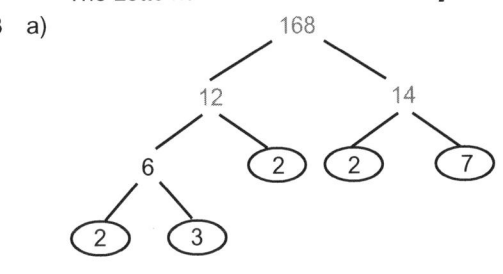

or

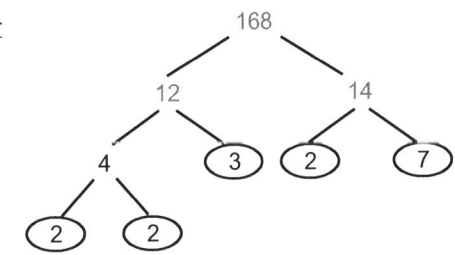

[2 marks available — 1 mark for finding the prime factors of 12, 1 mark for finding the prime factors of 14]

   b)   2 × 2 × 2 × 3 × 7 (or $2^3 \times 3 \times 7$) *[1 mark]*

Page 4 — LCM and HCF

1   Multiples of 6:   6, 12, ⑱ 24, 30, 36, 42, ...
      Multiples of 9:   9, ⑱ 27, 36, 45, 54, 63, ...
      So the LCM of 6 and 9 is 18. *[1 mark]*

2   Factors of 80:   1, 2, 4, 5, 8, 10, ⑯ 20, 40, 80
      Factors of 96:   1, 2, 3, 4, 6, 8, 12, ⑯ 24, 32, 48, 96
      So the HCF of 80 and 96 is 16. *[1 mark]*

3   Factors of 24:   1, 2, 3, 4, ⑥ 8, 12, 24
      Factors of 42:   1, 2, 3, ⑥ 7, 14, 21, 42
      Factors of 72:   1, 2, 3, 4, ⑥ 8, 9, 12, 18, 24, 36, 72
      So the HCF of 24, 42 and 72 is 6.
[2 marks available — 1 mark for using the correct method, 1 mark for the correct answer]

4   Multiples of 8:   8, 16, 24, 32, 40, 48, ㊷ 64, 72, 80, ...
      Multiples of 14: 14, 28, 42, ㊷ 70, ...
      So the drummers will play at the same time again after 56 beats.
[2 marks available — 1 mark for using the correct method, 1 mark for the correct answer]

Section 1 — Numbers

Answers: P5 — P8

Page 5 — Fractions, Decimals and Percentages

1

Fraction	Decimal	Percentage
$\frac{19}{100}$	0.19	19%
$\frac{83}{100}$	0.83	83%
$\frac{379}{1000}$	0.379	37.9%
$\frac{11}{16}$	0.6875	68.75%

[2 marks available — 2 marks for a fully correct table, otherwise 1 mark for two correct rows]

2 Change all numbers into the same form to compare them, e.g. percentages:

$0.12 = 12\%$, 17%, $\frac{1}{20} = \frac{5}{100} = 5\%$, $\frac{13}{100} = 13\%$, 9%

Now put them in order and change back into their original form:
5%, 9%, 12%, 13%, 17%
$\frac{1}{20}$, 9%, 0.12, $\frac{13}{100}$, 17%

[2 marks available — 1 mark for changing all the numbers into the same form, 1 mark for ordering them correctly]

3 a) $\frac{7}{50} = \frac{14}{100} = 14\%$ *[1 mark]*

b) $\frac{17}{20} = \frac{85}{100} = 85\%$ *[1 mark]*

c) $\frac{3}{25} = \frac{12}{100} = 12\%$ *[1 mark]*

To change fractions into percentages (without a calculator) the easiest thing to do is to find an equivalent fraction with 100 as the denominator. Then the numerator is your answer.

4 No, $\frac{1}{3}$ is not equal to 0.3, it equals 0.3333... *[1 mark]*

Pages 6-7 — Fractions

1 a) $\frac{16}{20} = \frac{4}{5}$ (÷4) *[1 mark]*

b) $\frac{24}{56} = \frac{3}{7}$ (÷8) *[1 mark]*

2 a) $\frac{2}{6} = \frac{4}{12} = \frac{8}{24} = \frac{16}{48} = \frac{32}{96}$ (×2) *[1 mark]*

Simplest form = $\frac{1}{3}$ *[1 mark]*

b) $\frac{6}{10} = \frac{12}{20} = \frac{24}{40} = \frac{48}{80} = \frac{96}{160}$ (×2) *[1 mark]*

Simplest form = $\frac{3}{5}$ *[1 mark]*

3 Change the mixed number into an improper fraction:

$2\frac{3}{7} = 2 + \frac{3}{7} = \frac{14}{7} + \frac{3}{7} = \frac{17}{7}$. So James is not correct as $\frac{17}{7}$ is not equal to $\frac{23}{7}$. *[1 mark]*

Or you could start with $\frac{23}{7}$ and convert it into a mixed number:
$\frac{23}{7} = \frac{21}{7} + \frac{2}{7} = 3 + \frac{2}{7} = 3\frac{2}{7}$, which is not equal to $2\frac{3}{7}$.

4 Georgina: $\frac{5}{8} = \frac{15}{24}$ (×3), Amie: $\frac{7}{12} = \frac{14}{24}$ (×2), Marcella: $\frac{3}{4} = \frac{18}{24}$ (×6)

Now that the denominators are the same, put the girls in order using the size of the numerators.
Amie, Georgina, Marcella

[2 marks available — 1 mark for putting the fractions over the same denominator, 1 mark for the correct answer]

5 a) $\frac{22}{9} - \frac{5}{6} = \frac{44}{18} - \frac{15}{18} = \frac{29}{18}$ *[1 mark]*

b) $\frac{5}{7} \div \frac{3}{13} = \frac{5}{7} \times \frac{13}{3} = \frac{65}{21}$ *[1 mark]*

6 a) $3\frac{5}{8} + 1\frac{7}{16} = \frac{29}{8} + \frac{23}{16} = \frac{58}{16} + \frac{23}{16} = \frac{81}{16} = 5\frac{1}{16}$ *[1 mark]*

b) $\frac{9}{10} \times 1\frac{11}{12} = \frac{9}{10} \times \frac{23}{12} = \frac{3}{10} \times \frac{23}{4} = \frac{69}{40} = 1\frac{29}{40}$ *[1 mark]*

c) $2\frac{5}{12} \div \frac{29}{24} = \frac{29}{12} \times \frac{24}{29} = \frac{1}{12} \times \frac{24}{1} = \frac{24}{12} = 2$ *[1 mark]*

7 a) $\frac{3}{10} \times £5.00 = (£5.00 \times 3) \div 10$
$= £15.00 \div 10 = £1.50$ *[1 mark]*

b) He spends $\frac{3}{10} + \frac{1}{4} + \frac{2}{5} = \frac{6}{20} + \frac{5}{20} + \frac{8}{20} = \frac{19}{20}$

So he saves $1 - \frac{19}{20} = \frac{1}{20}$ of his money.

$\frac{1}{20}$ of £5.00 = £5.00 ÷ 20 = £0.25

[2 marks available — 1 mark for using a correct method, 1 mark for correct answer]

You could also find the amounts he spends on magazines and toys, and subtract those and your answer to part a) from £5.

Page 8 — Percentage Basics

1 a) 10% of £300 = £300 ÷ 10 = £30
5% of £300 = £30 ÷ 2 = £15
35% = (3 × 10%) + 5%
35% of £300 = (3 × £30) + £15 = £105 *[1 mark]*

b) 50% of £15.00 = £15.00 ÷ 2 = £7.50
150% = 100% + 50%
150% of £15.00 = £15.00 + £7.50 = £22.50 *[1 mark]*

2 Maths test: $\frac{49}{60} \times 100 = 81.666...\%$

Science test: $\frac{75}{95} \times 100 = 78.947...\%$

Liane did better in her Maths test.

[2 marks available — 1 mark for converting the scores into percentages, 1 mark for the correct answer]

3 $\frac{64}{40} \times 100 = \frac{16}{10} \times 100 = 16 \times 10 = 160\%$ *[1 mark]*

Section 1 — Numbers

Answers: P8 — P13

4 To be better off choosing 13%, 13% of the employee's weekly wage should be more than £10.
Mr Patel: 13% of £78.10 = 0.13 × £78.10 = £10.153
Miss Dalton: 13% of £72.50 = 0.13 × £72.50 = £9.425
Mrs Ferrar: 13% of £84.60 = 0.13 × £84.60 = £10.998
So Mr Patel and Mrs Ferrar would be better off choosing 13%.
[2 marks available — 1 mark for working out 13% of each person's wage, 1 mark for the correct answer]

Page 9 — Rounding Numbers

1 a) 2.4 *[1 mark]*
b) 43.12 *[1 mark]*
c) 0.490 *[1 mark]*

2

	1 s.f.	2 s.f.	3 s.f.
5653	6000	5700	5650
0.3592	0.4	0.36	0.359
0.001596	0.002	0.0016	0.00160

[2 marks available — 1 mark for a completely correct table, otherwise 1 mark for two correct rows]

3 a) 68 000 *[1 mark]*
b) 68 390 *[1 mark]*
c) 68 400 *[1 mark]*

4 552 054 and 549 152 *[1 mark]*

Page 10 — Rounding Errors and Estimating

1 a) Actual value = 54.846
Rounded value = 55
Error = 55 − 54.846 = 0.154 *[1 mark]*
b) Actual value = 54.846
Rounded value = 54.85
Error = 54.85 − 54.846 = 0.004 *[1 mark]*

2 a) Upper limit = 116 + (1 ÷ 2) = 116.5 *[1 mark]*
Lower limit = 116 − (1 ÷ 2) = 115.5 *[1 mark]*
b) Upper limit = 1.25 + (0.01 ÷ 2) = 1.255 *[1 mark]*
Lower limit = 1.25 − (0.01 ÷ 2) = 1.245 *[1 mark]*
Add half the rounding unit to the rounded value to find the upper limit. Subtract half the rounding unit from the rounded value to get the lower limit.

3 Upper limit = 12 100 + (100 ÷ 2) = 12 150 *[1 mark]*
Lower limit = 12 100 − (100 ÷ 2) = 12 050 *[1 mark]*
12 050 ≤ x < 12 150 *[1 mark]*

4 $\frac{306.9 + 99.6}{5.2 \times 43} \approx \frac{300 + 100}{5 \times 40} = \frac{400}{200} = 2$
[2 marks available — 1 mark for rounding all values correctly, 1 mark for the correct answer]

Page 11 — Powers

1 a) $3^4 \times 3^5 = 3^{4+5} = 3^9$ *[1 mark]*
b) $(2^6)^3 = 2^{6 \times 3} = 2^{18}$ *[1 mark]*
c) $4^3 \div 4^{-6} = 4^{3-(-6)} = 4^{3+6} = 4^9$ *[1 mark]*

2 a) $\frac{(m^2)^4 \times m^3 \times 1^{65}}{m^0 \times (m^3)^3} = \frac{m^8 \times m^3 \times 1}{1 \times m^9} = \frac{m^{11}}{m^9} = m^2$ *[1 mark]*
When $m = 2$, $m^2 = 2^2 = 4$ *[1 mark]*
You could also substitute 2 in first and then simplify.

b) $\frac{(y^{-2}) \times (y^2)^5}{(y^2)^2 \times y^4} = \frac{y^{-2} \times y^{10}}{y^4 \times y^4} = \frac{y^8}{y^8} = y^0$ *[1 mark]*
For any value of y, $y^0 = 1$ so $3^0 = 1$ *[1 mark]*
You could also substitute 3 in first and then simplify.

3 a) From the table, $729 = 9^3$ and $6561 = 9^4$, so $729 \times 6561 = 9^3 \times 9^4 = 9^7 = 4\,782\,969$ *[1 mark]*
b) $\frac{43\,046\,721}{531\,441} = \frac{9^8}{9^6} = 9^2 = 81$ *[1 mark]*

Page 12 — Square Roots and Cube Roots

1 a) $\sqrt{142} = 11.9163... = 11.92$ (2 d.p.) *[1 mark]*
b) $\sqrt[3]{17.64} = 2.6031... = 2.60$ (2 d.p.) *[1 mark]*
c) $\sqrt[5]{187\,654} = 11.3415... = 11.34$ (2 d.p.) *[1 mark]*

2 a) 19 and -19 *[1 mark]*
b) 6.1 and -6.1 *[1 mark]*
c) 6.87 and -6.87 *[1 mark]*

3 a) $\sqrt[3]{400} = 7.36806...$ cm *[1 mark]*
= 7.37 cm (3 s.f.) *[1 mark]*
b) $\sqrt[3]{12\,680} = 23.31881...$ m *[1 mark]*
= 23.3 m (3 s.f.) *[1 mark]*
c) $\sqrt[3]{12} = 2.28942...$ mm *[1 mark]*
= 2.29 mm (3 s.f.) *[1 mark]*

4 The two square numbers either side of 132 are 121 and 144. *[1 mark]*
$\sqrt{121} = 11$ and $\sqrt{144} = 12$ so $\sqrt{132}$ must lie between 11 and 12. *[1 mark]*

Page 13 — Standard Form

1 a) 9.845×10^4 *[1 mark]*
b) 6.4×10^{-3} *[1 mark]*

2 a) Country: Canada *[1 mark]*
Population: $3.5 \times 10^7 = 35\,000\,000$ *[1 mark]*
b) To find people per km² divide the population by the area:
India: $\frac{1.2 \times 10^9}{3.3 \times 10^6} = 363.6363...$ people per km² *[1 mark]*
UK: $\frac{6.3 \times 10^7}{2.4 \times 10^5} = 262.5$ people per km² *[1 mark]*
363.6363... − 262.5 = 101.13636...
= 101 to the nearest whole number *[1 mark]*

3 a) 2.5×10^{-4} *[1 mark]*
b) $\frac{1}{40\,000} = \frac{1}{4000} \times \frac{1}{10} = \frac{2.5 \times 10^{-4}}{10} = 2.5 \times 10^{-5}$ *[1 mark]*
c) $\frac{1}{4000} + \frac{1}{40\,000} = (2.5 \times 10^{-4}) + (2.5 \times 10^{-5})$ *[1 mark]*
= $(2.5 \times 10^{-4}) + (0.25 \times 10^{-4})$ *[1 mark]*
= $(2.5 + 0.25) \times 10^{-4}$
= 2.75×10^{-4} *[1 mark]*
Alternatively, convert the fractions to decimals, add the decimals and then convert your answer into standard form.

Section 1 — Numbers

Answers: P14 — P17

Section 2 — Algebra

Pages 14-15 — Algebra

1. a) $4x - 2y + 3x + y = 4x + 3x - 2y + y = 7x - y$ *[1 mark]*
   b) $2x^2 - 2x + 6x - 5 - x^3 + 4x^2$
   $= -x^3 + 2x^2 + 4x^2 + 6x - 2x - 5$
   $= -x^3 + 6x^2 + 4x - 5$ *[1 mark]*

2. a) $2(5x - 1) = (2 \times 5x) + (2 \times -1) = 10x - 2$ *[1 mark]*
   b) $6x(4x - 3y) = (6x \times 4x) + (6x \times -3y) = 24x^2 - 18xy$ *[1 mark]*

3. a) $(x + 3)(x + 6) = x^2 + 6x + 3x + 18 = x^2 + 9x + 18$
   [2 marks available — 2 marks for correct answer, otherwise 1 mark for 2 terms correct]
   b) $(x - 4)(x + 9) = x^2 + 9x - 4x - 36 = x^2 + 5x - 36$
   [2 marks available — 2 marks for correct answer, otherwise 1 mark for 2 terms correct]

4. a) $(2x - 1)(x - 6) = 2x^2 - 12x - x + 6 = 2x^2 - 13x + 6$
   [2 marks available — 2 marks for correct answer, otherwise 1 mark for 2 terms correct]
   b) $(x + 4)^2 = (x + 4)(x + 4)$
   $= x^2 + 4x + 4x + 16 = x^2 + 8x + 16$
   [2 marks available — 2 marks for correct answer, otherwise 1 mark for 2 terms correct]

5. $(x - 2)(x + 1)(x + 4)$
   $= (x^2 + x - 2x - 2)(x + 4)$
   $= (x^2 - x - 2)(x + 4)$
   $= x^3 - x^2 - 2x + 4x^2 - 4x - 8 = x^3 + 3x^2 - 6x - 8$
   Multiplying any two brackets out first will give the same answer.
   [3 marks available — 3 marks for fully correct answer, otherwise 1 mark for multiplying out any two brackets correctly and 1 mark for 3 terms correct in final answer]

6. a) $12a + 18 = 6(2a + 3)$ *[1 mark]*
   b) $12ab + 6b^2 = 6(2ab + b^2)$
   $= 6b(2a + b)$
   [2 marks available — 2 marks for correct answer, otherwise 1 mark for correctly taking 1 factor outside the brackets]

7. a) $6xy - 10y = 2(3xy - 5y)$
   $= 2y(3x - 5)$
   [2 marks available — 2 marks for correct answer, otherwise 1 mark for correctly taking 1 factor outside the brackets]
   b) Area = Length × Width, so Width = $\dfrac{\text{Area}}{\text{Length}}$
   Substitute in what you know:
   Width = $\dfrac{2y(3x - 5)}{y}$ *[1 mark]*
   $= 2(3x - 5)$ or $6x - 10$ *[1 mark]*

8. a) $2x^2 - 4x = 2(x^2 - 2x)$
   $= 2x(x - 2)$
   [2 marks available — 2 marks for correct answer, otherwise 1 mark for correctly taking 1 factor outside the brackets]
   b) $3xy^2 - 5x^2y = x(3y^2 - 5xy)$
   $= xy(3y - 5x)$
   [2 marks available — 2 marks for correct answer, otherwise 1 mark for correctly taking 1 factor outside the brackets]

9. $15x^4y^3 + 5xy^3 + 10x^2y^4 = 5(3x^4y^3 + xy^3 + 2x^2y^4)$
   $= 5x(3x^3y^3 + y^3 + 2xy^4)$
   $= 5xy^3(3x^3 + 1 + 2xy)$
   [3 marks available — 3 marks for correct answer, otherwise 1 mark for correctly taking a factor outside the brackets or 2 marks for correctly taking 2 factors outside the brackets]

Pages 16-17 — Solving Equations

1. a) $2s + 1 = 5$
   $2s + 1 - 1 = 5 - 1$
   $2s = 4$ *[1 mark]*
   $2s \div 2 = 4 \div 2$
   $s = 2$ *[1 mark]*
   b) $3r - 5 = 4$
   $3r - 5 + 5 = 4 + 5$
   $3r = 9$ *[1 mark]*
   $3r \div 3 = 9 \div 3$
   $r = 3$ *[1 mark]*

2. a) $\dfrac{p - 7}{3} = 7$
   $\dfrac{p - 7}{3} \times 3 = 7 \times 3$
   $p - 7 = 21$ *[1 mark]*
   $p - 7 + 7 = 21 + 7$
   $p = 28$ *[1 mark]*
   b) $\dfrac{m}{3} + 2 = 6$
   $\dfrac{m}{3} + 2 - 2 = 6 - 2$
   $\dfrac{m}{3} = 4$ *[1 mark]*
   $\dfrac{m}{3} \times 3 = 4 \times 3$
   $m = 12$ *[1 mark]*

3. a) $230m = 23m \times 10$
   So, $230m = 184 \times 10$
   $= 1840$ *[1 mark]*
   b) $23(m + 2) = 23m + 23 \times 2 = 23m + 46$ *[1 mark]*
   From the question, $23m = 184$,
   so $23(m + 2) = 184 + 46 = 230$. *[1 mark]*

4. a) $2x + 8 = 4 - 6x$
   $2x + 8 - 8 = 4 - 6x - 8$
   $2x = -4 - 6x$ *[1 mark]*
   $2x + 6x = -4 - 6x + 6x$
   $8x = -4$
   $8x \div 8 = -4 \div 8$
   $x = -0.5$ *[1 mark]*
   b) $6(x - 1) = 42$
   $6(x - 1) \div 6 = 42 \div 6$
   $x - 1 = 7$ *[1 mark]*
   $x - 1 + 1 = 7 + 1$
   $x = 8$ *[1 mark]*

5. a) $4(x - 2) - 2(3 - 2x) = 5x + 1$
   $4x - 8 - 6 + 4x = 5x + 1$
   $8x - 14 = 5x + 1$ *[1 mark]*
   $8x - 14 + 14 = 5x + 1 + 14$
   $8x = 5x + 15$
   $8x - 5x = 5x + 15 - 5x$
   $3x = 15$ *[1 mark]*
   $3x \div 3 = 15 \div 3$
   $x = 5$ *[1 mark]*
   b) $\dfrac{6}{2x - 1} = 2$
   $\dfrac{6}{2x - 1} \times (2x - 1) = 2 \times (2x - 1)$
   $6 = 2(2x - 1)$ *[1 mark]*
   $6 = 4x - 2$ *[1 mark]*
   $6 + 2 = 4x - 2 + 2$
   $8 = 4x$
   $8 \div 4 = 4x \div 4$
   $x = 2$ *[1 mark]*

Section 2 — Algebra

Answers: P17 — P22

6    $\sqrt{1-2x} = 3$
     $(\sqrt{1-2x})^2 = 3^2$
     $1 - 2x = 9$ *[1 mark]*
     $1 - 2x - 1 = 9 - 1$
     $-2x = 8$ *[1 mark]*
     $-2x \div -2 = 8 \div -2$
     $x = -4$ *[1 mark]*

7    $\dfrac{3x-2}{8} = \dfrac{2x-1}{6}$
     $\dfrac{3x-2}{8} \times 8 = \dfrac{2x-1}{6} \times 8$
     $3x - 2 = \dfrac{8(2x-1)}{6}$
     $(3x - 2) \times 6 = \dfrac{8(2x-1)}{6} \times 6$
     $6(3x - 2) = 8(2x - 1)$ *[1 mark]*
     $18x - 12 = 16x - 8$
     $18x - 12 + 12 = 16x - 8 + 12$
     $18x = 16x + 4$ *[1 mark]*
     $18x - 16x = 16x + 4 - 16x$
     $2x = 4$
     $2x \div 2 = 4 \div 2$
     $x = 2$ *[1 mark]*

Page 18 — Using Formulas

1   a)   Substitute into formula: $T = \dfrac{155 \times 4 + 400}{5} = \dfrac{1020}{5}$
                    $= 204$ minutes *[1 mark]*

    b)   Substitute into formula: $W = \dfrac{5 \times 16.5}{11} = \dfrac{82.5}{11} = 7.5$ kg *[1 mark]*

         Then $T = \dfrac{155 \times 7.5 + 400}{5} = \dfrac{1562.5}{5}$
                      $= 312.5$ minutes *[1 mark]*

2   Substitute into formula:
     $d = (2 \times 10) + \dfrac{1}{2} \times 0.5 \times 10^2 = 45$ m
     [2 marks available — 2 marks for correct answer, otherwise 1 mark for correct substitution]

3   Substitute into formula:
     $H = (2 \times (-3)^2) + (2 \times 10.5) - \dfrac{(2 \times 10.5) + -3}{3 \times 2}$
        $= 18 + 21 - 3 = 36$
     [2 marks available — 2 marks for correct answer, otherwise 1 mark for correct substitution]

Pages 19-20 — Equations and Formulas from Words

1   a) $3T - 17 = 28$ *[1 mark]*
    b) $D = 46 - 2T$ *[1 mark]*

2   a) $P = 3x + 3x + x + 4 + x + 4$ *[1 mark]*
        $P = 8x + 8$ or $P = 8(x + 1)$ *[1 mark]*
    b) $A = 3x(x + 4)$ *[1 mark]*
        $A = 3x^2 + 12x$ *[1 mark]*

3   a) $(2x + 3)^2$ *[1 mark]*
    b) $(2x + 3)(2x + 3) = 4x^2 + 6x + 6x + 9$ *[1 mark]*
                            $= 4x^2 + 12x + 9$ *[1 mark]*

4   a) $T = 0.06c + 10$ *[1 mark]*
    b)   Substitute into formula: $16.48 = 0.06c + 10$
        $0.06c = 16.48 - 10 = 6.48$
        $c = 6.48 \div 0.06 = 108$
        [2 marks available — 2 marks for correct answer, otherwise 1 mark for correctly substituting into formula from part a)]

5   a)   E.g. $\dfrac{5x + 5x + 5x + 4.50 + 5.20 + 2.30}{3} = 24$
        [2 marks available — 2 marks for answer above or any equivalent answer, otherwise 1 mark for correct x terms]
    b) $\dfrac{15x + 12}{3} = 24$
        $15x + 12 = 24 \times 3 = 72$ *[1 mark]*
        $15x = 72 - 12 = 60$
        $x = 4$ *[1 mark]*

6   a) $\sqrt{x^2 + 7} = x + 1$
        [2 marks available — 2 marks for correct answer, otherwise 1 mark for either side of equation correct]
    b) $\sqrt{x^2 + 7} = x + 1$
        $x^2 + 7 = (x + 1)^2$
        $x^2 + 7 = x^2 + 2x + 1$
        $7 = 2x + 1$
        $6 = 2x$
        $x = 3$
        [3 marks available — 1 mark for correctly expanding $(x + 1)^2$, 1 mark for simplifying, 1 mark for correct answer]
        If you've got an equation to solve with a square root sign in it, the first thing to do is get rid of the square root sign by squaring both sides of the equation.

Page 21 — Rearranging Formulas

1   a) $F = 1.8C + 32$
        $F - 32 = 1.8C$ *[1 mark]*
        $C = \dfrac{F - 32}{1.8}$ *[1 mark]*
    b)   Substitute into formula: $\dfrac{80 - 32}{1.8} = \dfrac{48}{1.8} = 26.7$ °C (1 d.p) *[1 mark]*

2   a) $V = \dfrac{1}{3} \pi r^2 h$
        $3V = \pi r^2 h$ *[1 mark]*
        $h = \dfrac{3V}{\pi r^2}$ *[1 mark]*
    b) $V = \dfrac{1}{3} \pi r^2 h$
        $3V = \pi r^2 h$ *[1 mark]*
        $r^2 = \dfrac{3V}{\pi h}$ *[1 mark]*
        $r = \sqrt{\dfrac{3V}{\pi h}}$ *[1 mark]*

3    $d = st + \dfrac{1}{2} at^2$
     $2d = 2st + at^2$ *[1 mark]*
     $at^2 = 2d - 2st$
     $a = \dfrac{2d - 2st}{t^2}$ or $a = \dfrac{2(d - st)}{t^2}$ *[1 mark]*

Pages 22-23 — Number Patterns and Sequences

1   a) $1 - 4 = -3$, $-3 - 4 = -7$ *[1 mark for both correct]*
        The rule to get from one term to the next is "subtract 4".
    b) $7^2 = 49$, $8^2 = 64$ *[1 mark for both correct]*
        This is a sequence of square numbers.

Section 2 — Algebra

Answers: P22 — P25

2 To move from one pattern to the next you add a row of dots. The added row contains one more dot each time.

Pattern number	1	2	3	4	5	6	7	8
Number of dots	3	6	10	15	21	28	36	45

[2 marks available — 2 marks for all correct, otherwise 1 mark for 5 correct]

3 $4 \times 2 - 3 = 5$
$5 \times 2 - 3 = 7$
$7 \times 2 - 3 = 11$
$11 \times 2 - 3 = 19$
So the next four terms are 5, 7, 11, 19.
[2 marks available — 2 marks for all correct, otherwise 1 mark for 2 or 3 correct]

4 a) 2, 6, 10 *[1 mark]*
   b) $4n - 2 = 94$
      $4n = 96$
      $n = 24$, so 94 is the 24th term in the sequence.
      [2 marks available — 2 marks for correct answer, otherwise 1 mark for stating $4n - 2 = 94$]

5 There is a difference of 2 between each term in the sequence, so $2n$ is part of the nth term.
   Listing the values of $2n$, we have 2, 4, 6, 8...
   To get from $2n$ to the term we must add 6, so the nth term = $2n + 6$.
   [2 marks available — 2 marks for correct answer, otherwise 1 mark for getting $2n$]

6 The nth term of the sequence is $3n - 5$.
   $3n - 5 = 47$
   $3n = 52$ *[1 mark]*
   52 doesn't divide by 3 to give a whole number, so 47 is not in the sequence. *[1 mark]*

7 a) There is a difference of -6 between each term in the sequence, so $-6n$ is part of the nth term. *[1 mark]*
      Listing the values of $-6n$, we have -6, -12, -18, -24, -30... To get from $-6n$ to the term we must add 225, so the nth term = $225 - 6n$.
      [2 marks available — 2 marks for correct answer, otherwise 1 mark for getting $-6n$]
   b) $225 - 6n = -51$
      $-6n = -276$ *[1 mark]*
      $n = 46$
      So yes, -51 is a term in the sequence — it's the 46th term. *[1 mark]*

8 a)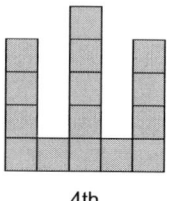
      4th *[1 mark]*
   b) n: 1 2 3 4
      number of tiles: 6 9 12 15
      There is a difference of 3 between each term in the sequence, so we have $3n$.
      Listing the values of $3n$, we have 3, 6, 9, 12...
      To get from $3n$ to the term we must add 3, so the nth term = $3n + 3$.
      [2 marks available — 2 marks for correct answer, otherwise 1 mark for $3n$]

Page 24 — Inequalities

1
	n = 3	n = 4	n = 5
n is greater than 4			✓
$3n$ is less than 15	✓	✓	
$n + 6$ is less than or equal to 9	✓		

[3 marks available — 1 mark for each correct row]

2 a) 2, 3 *[1 mark]*
   b) 3, 4, 5, 6 *[1 mark]*
   c) -2, -1, 0, 1 *[1 mark]*

3 $17 < x < 27$ *[1 mark]*
   $18 \leq x \leq 26$, $18 \leq x < 27$ and $17 < x \leq 26$ are also correct answers.

4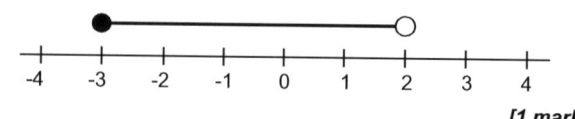
   [1 mark]

Section 3 — Graphs

Page 25 — X and Y Coordinates

1 a) A = (-2, 2)   B = (-4, -1)   C = (2, -1) *[1 mark]*
   b) Point D will have the same y-coordinate as point A and AD will be the same length as BC (6 units).

   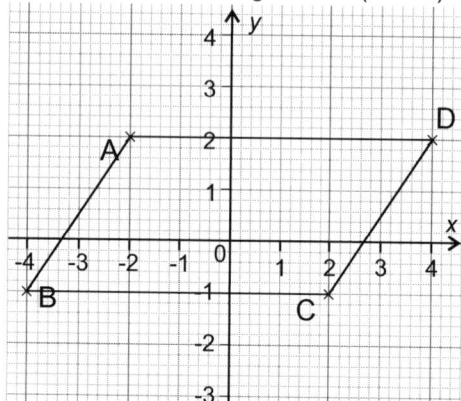

   D = (4, 2) *[1 mark]*
   c) base × vertical height = 6 × 3
      = 18 square units *[1 mark]*

2 a)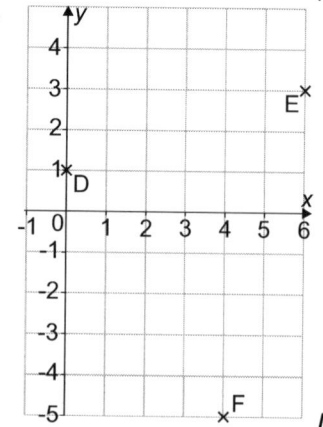
      [1 mark]
   b) x-coordinate = $\frac{0+6}{2} = 3$ y-coordinate = $\frac{1+3}{2} = 2$
      So midpoint of DE = (3, 2) *[1 mark]*

Section 3 — Graphs

Answers: P25 — P28

c) x-coordinate $= \frac{0+4}{2} = 2$ y-coordinate $= \frac{1+(-5)}{2} = -2$
So midpoint of DF = (2, -2) *[1 mark]*

Page 26 — Plotting Straight Line Graphs

1 a)
x	0	3	5
y	-2	7	13
[1 mark]

b)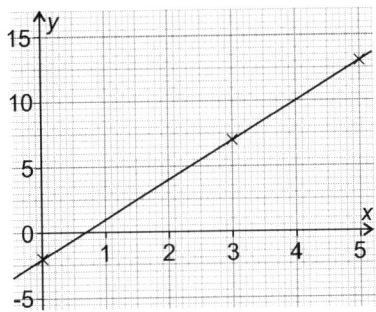
[1 mark]

c) Accept any answer with x-coordinate between 0.6 and 0.7, and y-coordinate = 0. *[1 mark]*
It actually crosses at (0.666..., 0), but you're not expected to be able to read a graph that accurately...

2 a) $y = 4 - x$ *[1 mark]*

b)
x	0	2	4
y	4	2	0
[1 mark]

c)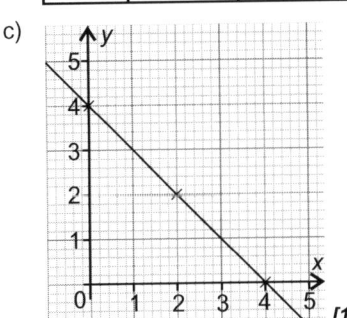
[1 mark]

Page 27 — Finding the Gradient

1 a)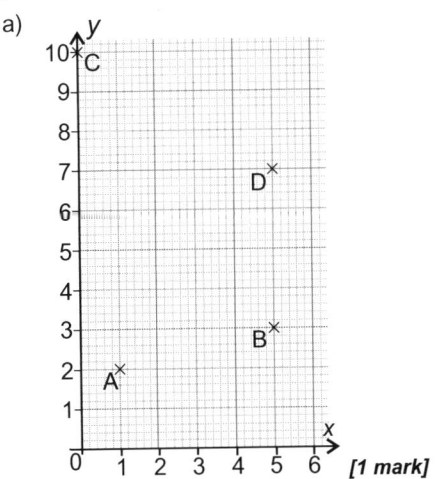
[1 mark]

b) $\frac{3-2}{5-1} = \frac{1}{4}$ *[1 mark]*

c) $\frac{7-10}{5-0} = \frac{-3}{5}$ *[1 mark]*

2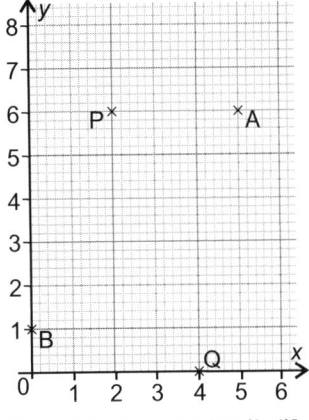

a) *[1 mark for B marked at (0, 1)]*
b) *[1 mark for Q marked at (4, 0)]*

3 Using the coordinates:
Gradient $= \frac{\text{Change in } y}{\text{Change in } x} = \frac{4a - 2a}{10 - 4} = \frac{2a}{6}$ *[1 mark]*

From question, gradient = 2, so:
$\frac{2a}{6} = 2$
$2a = 12$
$a = 6$ *[1 mark]*

Pages 28-29 — y = mx + c

1 Line AB: $y = 2$,   Line DA: $x = -2$,   Line AC: $y = -x$
[3 marks available — 1 mark for each correct equation]

2 $y = x + 5$ has gradient 1, y-intercept 5, so Line Q. *[1 mark]*

$y = 5x - 15$ has gradient 5 so Line T. *[1 mark]*
$5y = 2x + 40$ can be rearranged into the form $y = mx + c$ by dividing by 5:
$y = \frac{2x + 40}{5}$
This gives $y = \frac{2}{5}x + 8$ which has gradient $\frac{2}{5}$, y-intercept 8, so Line S. *[1 mark]*

3 a) Put $x = 0$ into each equation and see if it gives $y = -2$:
$x = 2y + 4$: $0 = 2y + 4$
              $-4 = 2y$ so $y = -2$ ✔
So $x = 2y + 4$ cuts the y-axis at $y = -2$ *[1 mark]*

b) Put $x = 2$ into each equation and see if it gives $y = 3$:
$x = 2y + 4$: $2 = 2y + 4$
              $-2 = 2y$ so $y = -1$ ✘
$2y = -3x + 12$: $2y = (-3 \times 2) + 12$
                $2y = -6 + 12$
                $2y = 6$ so $y = 3$ ✔
$2x = 2y - 4$: $2 \times 2 = 2y - 4$
              $4 = 2y - 4$
              $8 = 2y$ so $y = 4$ ✘
$3y = 11 - x$: $3y = 11 - 2$
              $3y = 9$ so $y = 3$ ✔

$2y = -3x + 12$ *[1 mark]* and $3y = 11 - x$ *[1 mark]*

Section 3 — Graphs

Answers: P29 — P33

4 a) The line will cut the y-axis at (0, 1) and have a gradient of 3.

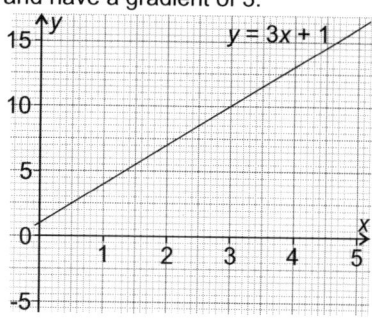
[1 mark]

b) The parallel line will have the same gradient as the first line and pass through (0, -3).

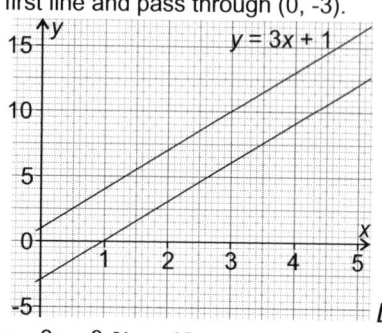
[1 mark]

c) $y = 3x - 3$ *[1 mark]*

5 a)

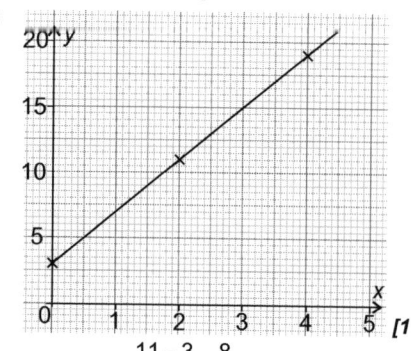
[1 mark]

b) Gradient = $\frac{11-3}{2-0} = \frac{8}{2} = 4$
y-intercept = 3
So a = 4 and b = 3 *[1 mark]*

c) The line will have the same gradient as the one in part b) so the equation of the parallel line will have the form: $y = 4x + c$. *[1 mark]*
Substitute in $x = 1$ and $y = 5$ to find the value for c:
$5 = (4 \times 1) + c$
$5 = 4 + c$
$c = 1$
So the equation of the parallel line is $y = 4x + 1$. *[1 mark]*

Pages 30-31 — Real-Life Graphs

1 a) 1 kg *[1 mark]*
The basic charge is the flat bit of the line.
b) 2.5 kg *[1 mark]*
c) One 5 kg parcel will cost £5.
Five 1 kg parcels will cost 5 × £2 = £10
So the difference is £10 – £5 = £5 *[1 mark]*

2 a) 15 minutes + 30 minutes = 45 minutes *[1 mark]*
b) 10:15 *[1 mark]*
c) 10:45 to 11:00 *[1 mark]*
The car was travelling fastest at the steepest part of its graph.

d) 50 miles *[1 mark]*
The van was travelling fastest between 12:00 and 13:00.

3 a) $128 *[1 mark]*
b) $128 – $80 = $48 *[1 mark]*
$48 = £30 *[1 mark]*

4 a) Graph C *[1 mark]*
The height increases as the lift goes up one floor. The graph then levels out when the lift stops. The height increases again as the lift goes up to the next floor, before levelling out again as the lift stops.
b) Graph A *[1 mark]*
The climber will not be climbing at a constant rate so the line will not be straight, but it will show an increase overall.
c) Graph B *[1 mark]*
The bath is being filled at a constant rate and the sides of the bath are vertical. The height will therefore increase at a constant rate, so the graph has a constant gradient.

Page 32 — Solving Simultaneous Equations

1 a)

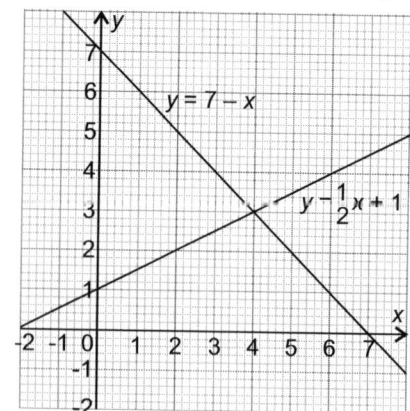

[2 marks available — 1 mark for drawing $y = \frac{1}{2}x + 1$ correctly, 1 mark for drawing $y = 7 - x$ correctly]

b) $x = 4, y = 3$ *[1 mark]*
These are the coordinates of the point where the lines cross.

2 a) $x = 2, y = 6$ *[1 mark]*
b) $x = 0, y = 4$ *[1 mark]*
c) $x = 1, y = 2$ *[1 mark]*

Page 33 — Quadratic Graphs

1 a)

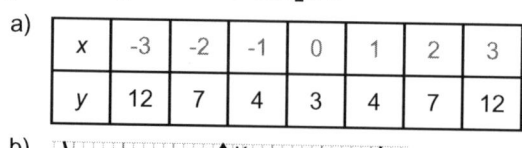
[1 mark]

b)

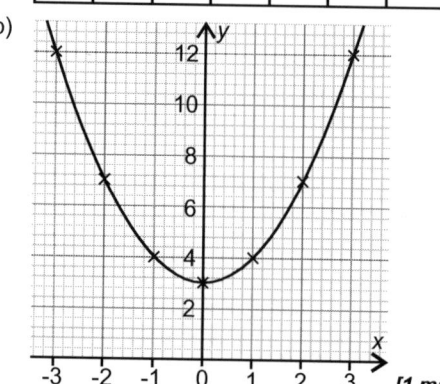
[1 mark]

c) -2.4 (allow -2.3 or -2.5) *[1 mark]*
and 2.4 (allow 2.3 or 2.5) *[1 mark]*

Section 3 — Graphs

Answers: P33 — P37

2 a)

x	-3	-2	-1	0	1	2	3
y	11	4	-1	-4	-5	-4	-1

[1 mark]

b)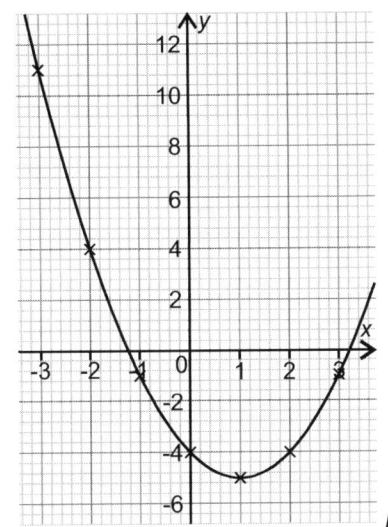
[1 mark]

c) x = -0.7 (allow -0.8 or -0.6) *[1 mark]*
and x = 2.7 (allow 2.6 or 2.8) *[1 mark]*

Section 4 — Ratio, Proportion and Rates of Change

Pages 34-35 — Ratios

1 a) ÷7 (21 : 56) ÷7
 = 3 : 8 *[1 mark]*

b) ÷4.5 (4.5 : 13.5) ÷4.5
 = 1 : 3 *[1 mark]*

c) 7 cm : 49 mm
 = 70 mm : 49 mm
 ÷7 = 10 mm : 7 mm ÷7
 = 10 : 7 *[1 mark]*

2 a) David: ÷2 (5 : 2) ÷2
 = 2.5 : 1
 Anna: ÷5 (11 : 5) ÷5
 = 2.2 : 1
 Laura: ÷4 (7 : 4) ÷4
 = 1.75 : 1
 [3 marks available — 1 mark for each correct ratio]

b) Laura *[1 mark]*
For every 1.75 races she runs, she wins one.

3 a) ×8 (9 : 5) ×8
 = 72 : 40
 So there are 40 crab sticks in the salad. *[1 mark]*

b) There are 72 − 8 = 64 prawns and 40 − 8 = 32 crab sticks in the remaining salad. *[1 mark]*
 ÷32 (64 : 32) ÷32
 = 2 : 1 *[1 mark]*

4 a) Total number of parts: 1 + 4 = 5
One part: 400 ÷ 5 = 80 trees. *[1 mark]*
There are 80 × 4 = 320 beech trees. *[1 mark]*

b) There are 400 ÷ 5 = 80 oak trees.
Oak trees account for 2 parts (in the new ratio), so 1 part is 80 ÷ 2 = 40 trees. *[1 mark]*
The number of beech trees in the new ratio will be 40 × 5 = 200. *[1 mark]*
So he should cut down 320 − 200 = 120 beech trees. *[1 mark]*

5 a) Scale up the ratio:
 ×3 (4 : 5) ×3
 = 12 : 15 *[1 mark]*
12 + 15 = 27 pupils *[1 mark]*

b) Scale up the ratio:
 ×4 (4 : 7) ×4
 = 16 : 28 *[1 mark]*
There are 28 pupils in the class and 16 are girls, so 28 − 16 = 12 are boys. *[1 mark]*

6 a) ÷5 (5 : 13) ÷5
 = 1 : 2.6
So there is 2.6 times more Y than X *[1 mark]*

b) 5 + 13 = 18 parts
144 ÷ 18 = 8 *[1 mark]*
8 × 13 = 104 g *[1 mark]*

c) ÷13 (5 : 13) ÷13
 = 0.3846... : 1 So for every gram of Y there are 0.38 (2 d.p) grams of X. *[1 mark]*

Page 36 — Direct Proportion

1 a) £10.80 ÷ 5 = £2.16 per notebook *[1 mark]*
£2.16 × 3 = £6.48 *[1 mark]*

b) £11.25 ÷ 15 = £0.75 per pen *[1 mark]*
£0.75 × 34 = £25.50 *[1 mark]*

2 a) 480 ÷ 5 = 96 calls per worker *[1 mark]*
96 × 12 = 1152 *[1 mark]*

b) Put the numbers you know in for c and w:
480 = 5k
k = 480 ÷ 5 = 96 *[1 mark]*
So the equation is $c = 96w$. *[1 mark]*

3 a) i) 30 g ÷ 8 = 3.75 g in one sachet
44 × 3.75 g = 165 g *[1 mark]*
ii) 8 sachets: 30 + 30 + 10 + 5 + 10 = 85 g
1 sachet: 85 g ÷ 8 = 10.625 g *[1 mark]*
44 sachets: 10.625 g × 44 = 467.5 g *[1 mark]*

b) 10 ÷ 8 = 1.25 g in one sachet *[1 mark]*
25 ÷ 1.25 = 20 sachets *[1 mark]*

Page 37 — Inverse Proportion

1 a) 1 × 4 = 4 hours for 1 window cleaner *[1 mark]*
4 ÷ 2 = 2 hours for 2 window cleaners *[1 mark]*

b) 4 ÷ 6 = $\frac{2}{3}$ hours for 6 window cleaners *[1 mark]*
$\frac{2}{3}$ hours = (60 ÷ 3) × 2 = 20 × 2 = 40 minutes *[1 mark]*

2 a) It would take 3 × 20 = 60 minutes at 1 mph. *[1 mark]*
So at 30 mph it would take 60 ÷ 30 = 2 minutes. *[1 mark]*

b) It would take 1 minute at 3 × 20 = 60 mph. *[1 mark]*
So it would take 12 minutes at 60 ÷ 12 = 5 mph. *[1 mark]*

Answers: P37 — P42

3 a) Put the numbers you know in for p and a:
$7000 = \dfrac{k}{3}$
$k = 21\,000$ *[1 mark]*
So the equation is $p = \dfrac{21000}{a}$ *[1 mark]*

b) $p = \dfrac{21000}{7} = £3000$ *[1 mark]*

Pages 38-39 — Percentage Change

1. $25\% = 0.25$
$0.25 \times 560 = 140$ extra customers
$560 + 140 = 700$ *[1 mark]*
You could also use the multiplier method:
$560 \times 1.25 = 700$.

2. $18\% = 0.18$
$0.18 \times £920 = £165.60$
$£920 - £165.60 = £754.40$ *[1 mark]*
Or, using the multiplier method, $£920 \times 0.82 = £754.40$.

3. a) $5\% = 0.05$
$0.05 \times £300 = £15$
$£15 \times 3 = £45$ *[1 mark]*
b) $5.5\% = 0.055$
$0.055 \times £400 = £22$
$£22 \times 5 = £110$ *[1 mark]*
$£400 + £110 = £510$ *[1 mark]*

4. a) Profit: $£4400 - £4000 = £400$ *[1 mark]*
$(400 \div 4000) \times 100 = 0.1 \times 100 = 10\%$ profit *[1 mark]*
b) Loss: $£4000 - £3500 = £500$ *[1 mark]*
$(500 \div 4000) \times 100 = 0.125 \times 100 = 12.5\%$ loss *[1 mark]*

5. a) $1.7 - 1.25 = 0.45$ m increase *[1 mark]*
$\dfrac{0.45}{1.25} \times 100 = 36\%$ *[1 mark]*
b) $36 \div 2 = 18\% = 0.18$
$0.18 \times 1.7 = 0.306$ *[1 mark]*
$1.7 + 0.306 = 2.006$
$= 2.01$ metres (to the nearest cm) *[1 mark]*

6. Single bed: $£63.75 = 85\%$
$£0.75 = 1\%$
$£75.00 = 100\%$
Double bed: $£240 = 60\%$
$£4 = 1\%$
$£400 = 100\%$
Bunk Beds: $£168 = 80\%$
$£2.10 = 1\%$
$£210 = 100\%$

ITEM	SALE PRICE	DISCOUNT	ORIGINAL PRICE
Single bed	£63.75	15%	£75
Double bed	£240	40%	£400
Bunk beds	£168	20%	£210

[3 marks available — 1 mark for each correct original price]
You can also use the multiplier method,
e.g. original price of single bed = $£63.75 \div 0.85 = £75$.

7. Original price: $£2805 = 82.5\%$
$£34 = 1\%$
$£3400 = 100\%$
OR: Original price = $£2805 \div 0.825 = £3400$.
$£3400 - £2805 = £595$
[2 marks available — 1 mark for finding original price, 1 mark for finding amount lost]

Page 40 — Converting Units

1. a) 1 kg = 1000 g so the conversion factor is 1000.
$374 \div 1000 = 0.347$ kg *[1 mark]*
b) 1 cm = 10 mm so the conversion factor is 10.
$20.2 \times 10 = 202$ mm *[1 mark]*

2. 1 yard = 3 feet so the conversion factor is 3.
22 yards = $22 \times 3 = 66$ feet *[1 mark]*
1 foot = 12 inches so the conversion factor is 12.
66 feet = $66 \times 12 = 792$ inches *[1 mark]*

3. a) 1 kg ≈ 2.2 lb so the conversion factor is 2.2.
$33 \div 2.2 = 15$ so 33 lb ≈ 15 kg *[1 mark]*
b) 1 stone = 14 lb so the conversion factor is 14.
3 stone 2 lb = $(3 \times 14) + 2 = 44$ lb *[1 mark]*
Total weight loss = $44 + 33 = 77$ lb
77 lb ≈ $77 \div 2.2 = 35$ kg *[1 mark]*
You could also convert 44lb to kg, then add it to your answer from part a) to get the result.

4. a) 1 gallon ≈ 4.5 litres so the conversion factor is 4.5.
$12 \times 4.5 = 54$ so 12 gallons ≈ 54 litres *[1 mark]*
b) 1 foot ≈ 30 cm so the conversion factor is 30.
$16 \times 30 = 480$ so 16 feet ≈ 480 cm *[1 mark]*
480 cm = 4.8 m
So yes, the car will be able to fit into Mr Roe's garage. *[1 mark]*

Page 41 — More Conversions

1. a) $4.6 \times 100 \times 100 = 46\,000$ cm^2 *[1 mark]*
b) $300 \div (10 \times 10) = 3$ cm^2 *[1 mark]*
c) $10 \div (100 \times 100) = 0.001$ m^2 *[1 mark]*

2. Amount of squash in each jug:
$0.003 \times 100 \times 100 \times 100 = 3000$ cm^3 *[1 mark]*
Total amount of squash: $3000 \times 3 = 9000$ cm^3 *[1 mark]*
$9000 \div 200 = 45$ cups *[1 mark]*

3. Speed of the car: $130 \times 1.6 = 208$ km/h *[1 mark]*
The motorbike only had an average speed of 200 km/h so the car won the race. *[1 mark]*
You could also change the motorbike's speed into mph and then compare the speeds.

4. There are $60 \times 60 = 3600$ seconds in an hour.
$0.02 \times 3600 = 72$ km/h
[2 marks available — 1 mark for a correct method, 1 mark for the correct answer]

Page 42 — Maps and Scale Drawings

1. a) The distance from the Banyan Tree to the castle is 5 cm.
Real-life distance = $5 \times 4 = 20$ km *[1 mark]*
b) The distance from the Misty Mountain to the Hidden Caves is 2.7 cm.
Real-life distance = $2.7 \times 4 = 10.8$ km *[1 mark]*

Section 4 — Ratio, Proportion and Rates of Change

Answers: P42 — P45

c) The treasure is 6 ÷ 4 = 1.5 cm from Misty Mountain.

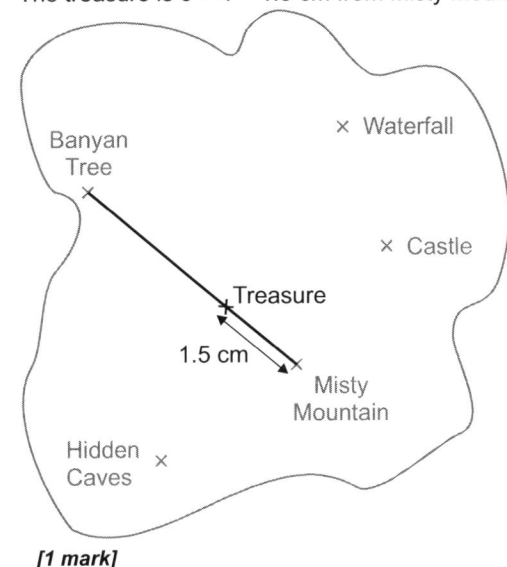

[1 mark]

2 a) Real-life length: 9 × 50 = 450 cm *[1 mark]*
= 4.5 m *[1 mark]*

b) Length of model: 11 ÷ 50 = 0.22 m *[1 mark]*
= 22 cm *[1 mark]*

3 The dimensions of the rug are 0.5 cm × 5 cm.
Real-life dimensions of the rug:
0.5 × 100 = 50 cm = 0.5 m *[1 mark]*
and 5 × 100 = 500 cm = 5 m *[1 mark]*
Area = 0.5 × 5 = 2.5 m² *[1 mark]*
Alternatively you could work out the area of the rug in the scale drawing and then convert the area to real life.

Page 43 — Best Buy

1 Bronze: 40 ÷ 5 = 8p per sticker
Silver: £1.20 ÷ 20 = £0.06 = 6p per sticker
Gold: £3.50 ÷ 50 = £0.07 = 7p per sticker
So the best value for money is the Silver pack.
[3 marks available — 1 mark for finding the price per sticker for two of the packs, 1 mark for finding it for the third pack, 1 mark for the correct answer]
Alternatively you could find the amount per penny and compare.

2 A: 568 ml ÷ 37p = 15.3513... ml per penny
B: 2 litres = 2000 ml and £1.27 = 127p
2000 ml ÷ 127p = 15.7480... ml per penny
C: 3.25 litres = 3250 ml and £2.03 = 203p
3250 ml ÷ 203p = 16.0098... ml per penny
C is the best option because you got the most milk per penny.
[3 marks available — 1 mark for finding the ml per penny for two of the bottles, 1 mark for finding it for the third bottle, 1 mark for the correct answer]
Alternatively you could find the price per ml and compare.

3 a) Cheddar & Sons:
£7.58 = 758 p
800 g ÷ 758 p = 1.05540... g per penny
Cheesetastic Cheddar:
2 kg = 2000g and £19.19 = 1919 p
2000 g ÷ 1919 p = 1.04220... g per penny
Cheddar & Sons is the best value because you get more cheese per penny.
[2 marks available — 1 mark for finding the grams per penny of the two cheeses, 1 mark for the correct answer]
Alternatively you could find the price per g and compare.

b) Cheddar & Sons is better value (from part a).
4 kg = 4000 g
4000 g ÷ 800 g = 5 packs are needed
£7.58 × 5 = £37.90 *[1 mark]*
£50 − £37.90 = £12.10 *[1 mark]*

Page 44 — Density and Speed

1 a) Density = 300 ÷ 0.02 = 15 000 kg/m³ *[1 mark]*
b) Density = 1620 ÷ 0.6 = 2700 kg/m³ *[1 mark]*

2 From 8 am to 1.30 pm there are
5 hours and 30 minutes = 5.5 hours *[1 mark]*
Distance = 70 × 5.5 = 385 km *[1 mark]*

3 Volume = 124.8 kg ÷ 0.832 kg/litre = 150 litres *[1 mark]*
Cost = 150 × £1.36 = £204 *[1 mark]*

4 If he leaves at 3 pm and needs to be there at 5 pm he has 2 hours to get to the airport. *[1 mark]*
The airport is 200 ÷ 1.6 = 125 miles away. *[1 mark]*
At 60 mph it will take him 125 ÷ 60 = 2.0833... hours to get to the airport, which is more than 2 hours, so he won't make it to the airport on time. *[1 mark]*

Section 5 — Geometry and Measures

Page 45 — Symmetry and 2D Shapes

1

Name of shape	Number of lines of symmetry	Order of rotational symmetry
Isosceles Triangle	1	1
Parallelogram	0	2
Kite	1	1

[3 marks available — 1 mark for each fully correct row]

2 a) Regular heptagon *[1 mark]*
b) 7 *[1 mark]*
c) 7 *[1 mark]*

3

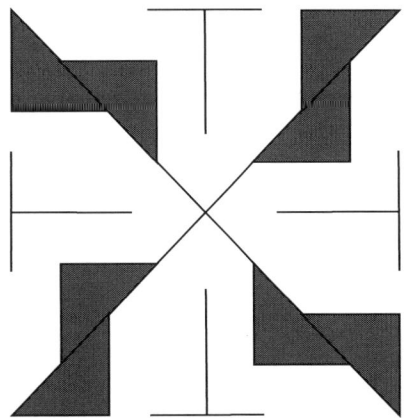

[2 marks available — 1 mark for adding triangles to the centre of the lines pointing clockwise, 1 mark for adding triangles at the ends of the lines pointing anticlockwise]

Answers: P46 — P50

Page 46 — Perimeter and Area

1. 4 + 9 + 5 + 3 + 2 + 4 + 3 + 2 = 32 cm *[1 mark]*
   The missing side on the diagram is 9 − 4 − 3 = 2 m.

2. 8 × 5 = 40 cm *[1 mark]*

3. $\frac{1}{2}$(13 + 9) × 6 = $\frac{1}{2}$ × 22 × 6 = 11 × 6 = 66 cm²
   [2 marks available — 1 mark for using the correct method, 1 mark for the correct answer]

4. Split the shape into two parallelograms, each with height of 4 cm. Then each parallelogram has an area of 9 × 4 = 36 cm². *[1 mark]*
   So the area of the shape is 36 × 2 = 72 cm². *[1 mark]*

Page 47 — Area

1. Area of the triangle = $\frac{1}{2}$ × 8 × 3 = 12 m²
   Area of the rectangle = 8 × (10 − 3)
   = 8 × 7 = 56 m²
   Area of the side of the house = 56 + 12
   = 68 m²
   [2 marks available — 1 mark for finding the area of the triangle and rectangle, 1 mark for the correct answer]

2. Area of triangle ADE = $\frac{1}{2}$ × 6 × 3 = 9 cm²
   Area of parallelogram ABCD = 6 × 4 = 24 cm²
   Area of pentagon = 24 + 9 = 33 cm²
   [2 marks available — 1 mark for finding the area of the triangle and parallelogram, 1 mark for the correct answer]

3. Find the height, *h*, of the triangle:
   $\frac{1}{2}$(7 × *h*) = 14
   7*h* = 28
   h = 4 cm *[1 mark]*
   The height of the trapezium is 4 cm too. So the area is:
   A = $\frac{1}{2}$(7 + 3) × 4 *[1 mark]*
   A = 5 × 4 = 20 cm² *[1 mark]*

Page 48 — Circles

1. Radius = 80 ÷ 2 = 40 cm *[1 mark]*
   Area = π × 40² = 5026.54824... cm²
   = 5026.55 cm² (2 d.p.) *[1 mark]*

2. Diameter = 1.6 × 2 = 3.2 m *[1 mark]*
   Circumference = 3.2 × π = 10.05309... m
   = 10.05 m (2 d.p.) *[1 mark]*

3. Area of big circle = 3² × π = 28.27433... cm² *[1 mark]*
   Area of small circle = 7.06858... cm² *[1 mark]*
   Area of rectangle = 25 × 8 = 200 cm²
   Area of remaining metal:
   200 − 28.27433... − 7.06858... = 164.65708... cm²
   = 164.66 cm² *[1 mark]*

Page 49 — 3D Shapes and Nets

1.
Shape	Name of shape	Number of vertices	Number of edges	Number of faces
	Square-Based Pyramid	5	8	5
	Cuboid	8	12	6
	Triangular Prism	6	9	5

[3 marks available — 1 mark for each correct row]

2. a) Cuboid *[1 mark]*
   b) and c)

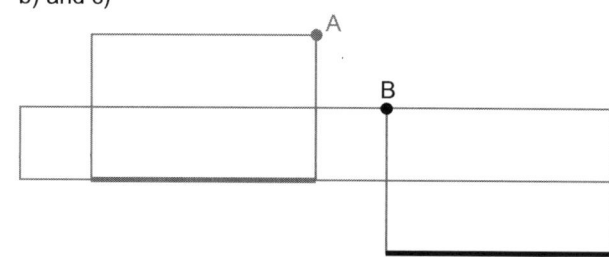

[1 mark for marking point B correctly]
[1 mark for drawing the bold line on the correct edge]

Page 50 — Nets and Surface Area

1. a) E.g.

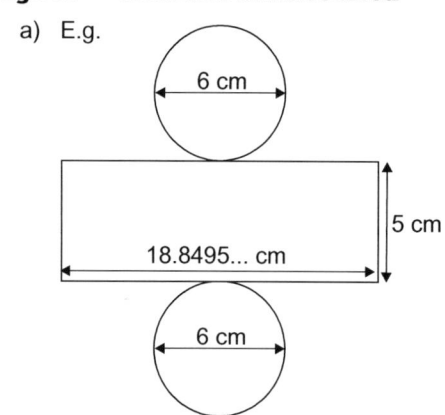

[2 marks available — 1 mark for drawing the correct net, 1 mark for labelling the diameter of the circles and both sides of the rectangle]

   b) Radius of each circle = 6 ÷ 2 = 3 cm
   Area of each circle = π × 3² = 28.27433... cm²
   Area of rectangle = 5 × 6π = 94.24777... cm²
   Total surface area:
   (28.27433... × 2) + 94.24777... = 150.79644... cm²
   = 150.80 (2 d.p.) cm²
   [3 marks available — 1 mark for finding the area of the circle, 1 mark for finding the area of the rectangle, 1 mark for the total surface area]

Section 5 — Geometry and Measures

Answers: P50 — P54

2 a) E.g.

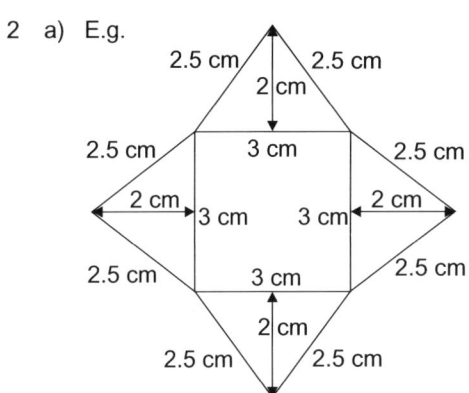

[2 marks available — 1 mark for drawing the correct net, 1 mark for labelling it correctly]

b) Area of square = 3 × 3 = 9 cm²

Area of each triangle = $\frac{1}{2}$ × 2 × 3 = 3 cm²

Surface area = 9 + (4 × 3) = 21 cm²

[2 marks available — 1 mark for finding the areas of the square and triangles, 1 mark for the correct answer]

Page 51 — Volume

1 18 × 6 = 108 cm³ *[1 mark]*
2 0.5 × 0.8 × 2.4 = 0.96 m³ *[1 mark]*
3 a) Radius = 7.4 ÷ 2 = 3.7 cm
   Cross-section = π × 3.7² = 43.00840... cm²
   = 43.01 cm² (2 d.p.) *[1 mark]*
   b) 43.00840... × 11 = 473.09243... cm³
   = 473.09 cm³ (2 d.p.) *[1 mark]*
4 You can fit 20 ÷ 5 = 4 bricks along the length, width and height of the box *[1 mark]*. So you can fit 4 × 4 × 4 = 64 bricks in the box. *[1 mark]*

Page 52 — Geometry Rules

1 a = 180° − 60° − 40° = 80° *[1 mark]*
   b = 180° − 25° − 80° = 75° *[1 mark]*
2 c = 180° − 40° = 140° *[1 mark]*
   One angle in the triangle is 90° and the other two angles are equal because the triangle is isosceles.
   So, d = (180° − 90°) ÷ 2 = 90° ÷ 2 = 45° *[1 mark]*
   e = 360° − 45° = 315° *[1 mark]*
3 a) ∠ACB = 180° − 90° − 24° = 66° *[1 mark]*
   b) ∠DCE = 180° − 80° − 66° = 34° *[1 mark]*
   c) ∠DEC = 180° − (2 × 34°) = 112° *[1 mark]*
4 x = 180° − 100° − 30° = 50° *[1 mark]*
   The two angles in the triangle with y are:
   40° and 180° − 100° − 50° = 30°, so
   y = 180° − 40° − 30° = 110° *[1 mark]*
   The unlabelled angle in the quadrilateral is,
   180° − 40° = 140°, so
   z = 360° − 130° − 140° − 50° = 40° *[1 mark]*

Page 53 — Parallel Lines

1 a) ∠BEF = 180° − 110° = 70° because it is an allied angle with the 110° angle. *[1 mark]*
   b) ∠DEC = 70° because it's vertically opposite ∠BEF.
   ∠ACB = ∠DCE = 180° − 52° − 70° = 58° because angles in a triangle add up to 180°.
   [2 marks available — 1 mark for finding ∠DEC with a suitable reason, 1 mark for finding ∠ACB with a suitable reason]

2 a)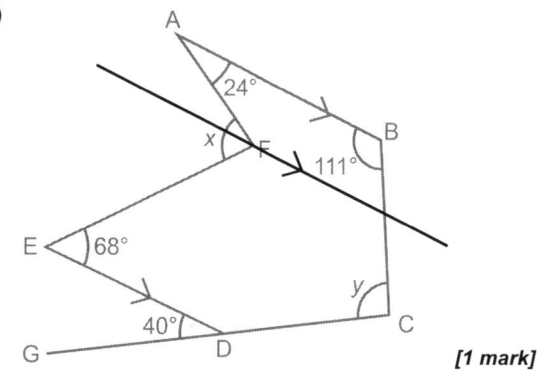
   [1 mark]

   b) x is made up from two alternate angles, one is alternate to 24° and the other to 68°. *[1 mark]*
   x = 24° + 68° = 92° *[1 mark]*

   c) By drawing a line parallel to AB and ED (going through C), you can split y into two angles.
   One angle is allied with ∠ABC so is 180° − 111° = 69°.
   The other is a corresponding angle with ∠EDG so is 40°.
   So, y = 69 + 40 = 109°.
   [2 marks available — 1 mark for splitting y into two angles and finding the value for each angle, 1 mark for the correct answer]

Page 54 — Interior and Exterior Angles

1 a) 360 ÷ 7 = 51.42857...° = 51.4° *[1 mark]*
   b) 180° − 51.42857...° = 128.57142...° = 128.6° *[1 mark]*
   c) 128.57142... × 7 = 900° *[1 mark]*
   Alternatively, (7 − 2) × 180° = 900°.
2 (20 − 2) × 180° = 18 × 180° = 3240°
   [2 marks available — 1 mark for using the correct formula, 1 mark for the correct answer]
3 Sum of the interior angles of an octagon:
   (8 − 2) × 180° *[1 mark]*
   = 6 × 180° = 1080° *[1 mark]*
   x = 1080° − 110° − 95° − 164° − 143°
   − 119° − 99° − 127° = 223° *[1 mark]*

Section 5 — Geometry and Measures

Answers: P55 — P59

Pages 55-56 — Transformations

1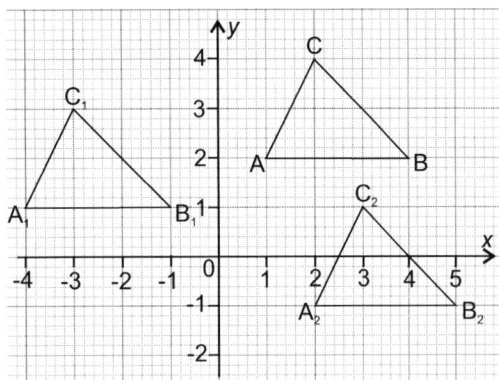

a) *[1 mark for triangle A₁B₁C₁ drawn in the correct position]*
b) *[1 mark for triangle A₂B₂C₂ drawn in the correct position]*
c) $\binom{1}{-3}$ *[1 mark]*

2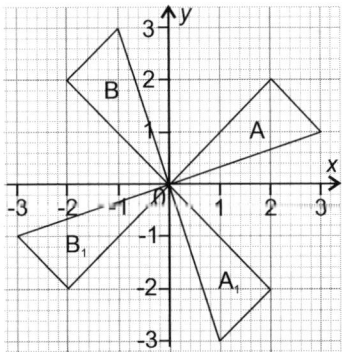

a) *[1 mark for shape A₁ drawn in the correct position]*
b) *[1 mark for shape B₁ drawn in the correct position]*
c) Rotation 90° anticlockwise about the origin
[2 marks available — 1 mark for '90° anticlockwise', 1 mark for 'about the origin' or 'about point (0, 0)']
You could also say rotation 270° clockwise about the origin.

3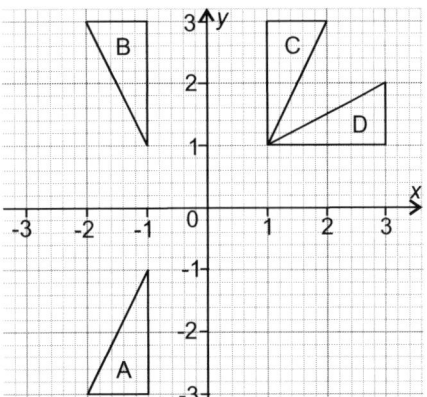

a) *[1 mark for shape B drawn in the correct position]*
b) *[1 mark for shape C drawn in the correct position]*
c) *[1 mark for shape D drawn in the correct position]*
d) Reflection in the line y = -x.
[2 marks available — 1 mark for saying it's a reflection, 1 mark for the equation of the mirror line]

4 a) i) 3 ÷ 2 = 1.5 *[1 mark]*
Divide a side length on B by the corresponding side length on A.
ii) (9, 1) *[1 mark]*
Draw lines through corresponding vertices of shapes A and B — the lines cross at the centre of enlargement.

b) Enlargement by scale factor $\frac{1}{2}$ with centre of enlargement (9, 7).
[2 marks available — 1 mark for the correct scale factor, 1 mark for the correct centre of enlargement]

Page 57 — Congruent Shapes

1 a) B and E *[1 mark]*
b) D *[1 mark]*

2 a) Not congruent — corresponding sides on the triangles are different lengths. *[1 mark]*
b) Congruent — two sides and the angle between them are equal on both triangles, so the SAS condition is satisfied. *[1 mark]*

3 B and D *[1 mark]*
Both triangles are right-angled, have a 5 cm hypotenuse and a 3 cm side. The RHS condition is therefore satisfied. *[1 mark]*
The missing angle in B is 180° − 53° − 37° = 90° so it's a right-angled triangle.

Page 58 — Similar Shapes

1 a) E *[1 mark]*
b) 2 *[1 mark]*
D is a regular heptagon, and so are B and F.

2 a) $\frac{15}{10} = \frac{3}{2}$ *[1 mark]*
b) 43 mm × $\frac{3}{2}$ = 64.5 mm *[1 mark]*
c) 9 mm ÷ $\frac{3}{2}$ = 6 mm *[1 mark]*
d) 50° *[1 mark]*

Page 59 — Constructions

1 a)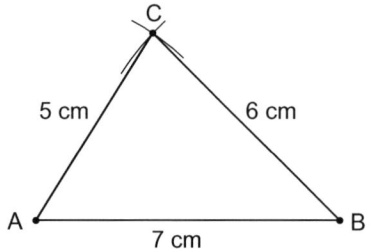

[2 marks available — 1 mark for correctly drawn construction arcs, 1 mark for a correct and accurate triangle]

b)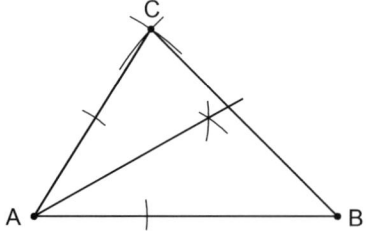

[2 marks available — 1 mark for correctly drawn construction arcs, 1 mark for a correct and accurate angle bisector]

Section 5 — Geometry and Measures

Answers: P59 — P63

2 a)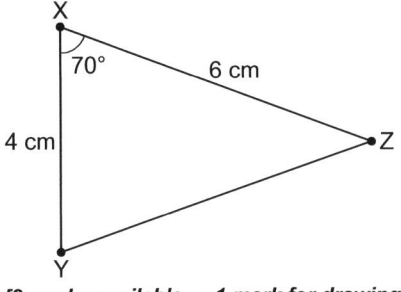

[2 marks available — 1 mark for drawing the 70° angle correctly, 1 mark for completing the triangle with XZ = 6 cm]

b)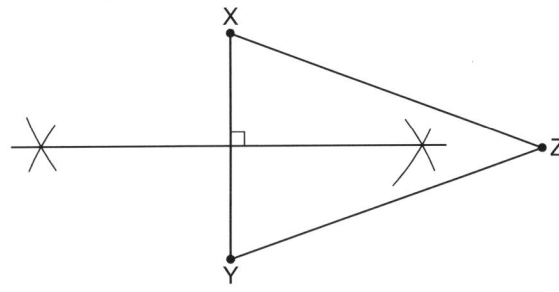

[2 marks available — 1 mark for correctly drawn construction arcs, 1 mark for a correct and accurate perpendicular bisector]

3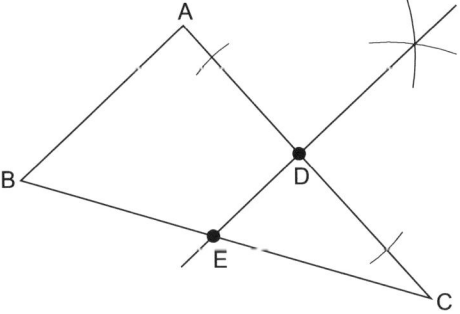

a) *[2 marks available — 1 mark for correctly drawn construction arcs, 1 mark for a correct and accurate perpendicular to AC at point D]*

b) 34 mm *[1 mark for any answer from 33 mm to 35 mm]*

Page 60 — Pythagoras' Theorem

1 1st triangle: $x^2 = 12^2 + 10^2 = 244$
$x = \sqrt{244} = 15.62049...$ m *[1 mark]*
2nd triangle: $17^2 = y^2 + 8^2$
$y^2 = 17^2 - 8^2 = 225$
$y = \sqrt{225} = 15$ m *[1 mark]*
So yes, Mike is correct, side x is longer than side y.
[1 mark]

2 Make a sketch of the triangle:

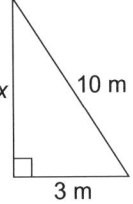 10 m

3 m

$10^2 = x^2 + 3^2$ *[1 mark]*
$x^2 = 10^2 - 3^2 = 91$
$x = \sqrt{91} = 9.539392...$ m = 9.54 m (3 s.f.) *[1 mark]*

3 Split the triangle into two right-angled triangles:

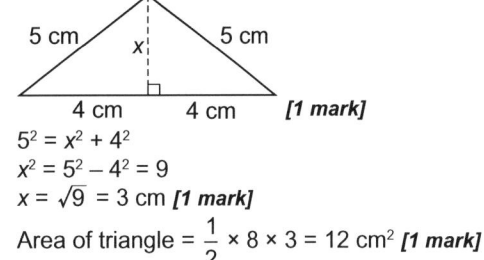

[1 mark]
$5^2 = x^2 + 4^2$
$x^2 = 5^2 - 4^2 = 9$
$x = \sqrt{9} = 3$ cm *[1 mark]*
Area of triangle = $\frac{1}{2} \times 8 \times 3 = 12$ cm² *[1 mark]*

Pages 61-62 — Trigonometry

1 $x = \tan 32° \times 20$ *[1 mark]*
$= 0.62486... \times 20$
$= 12.49738... = 12.5$ cm (1 d.p.) *[1 mark]*

2 Call the length of the ramp x:
$x = \dfrac{3}{\sin 15°}$ *[1 mark]*
$= 11.5911...$ m $= 11.6$ m (1 d.p.) *[1 mark]*

3 $\sin x = \dfrac{1.5}{2.6}$ *[1 mark]*
$\sin x = 0.5769...$
$x = \sin^{-1}(0.5769...) = 35.2344...° = 35.2°$ (1 d.p.) *[1 mark]*

4 a) BC = $\dfrac{1.5}{\cos 47°}$ *[1 mark]*
$= 2.1994...$ m $= 2.20$ m (2 d.p.) *[1 mark]*

b) $(2.1994... \times 2) + 3 = 7.3988...$ m
$= 7.40$ m (2 d.p.) *[1 mark]*

5 a) $\tan x = \dfrac{100}{160}$ *[1 mark]*
$\tan x = 0.625$
$x = \tan^{-1}(0.625) = 32.0053...° = 32.0°$ (1 d.p.) *[1 mark]*

b) $a = \dfrac{100}{\cos 40°}$ *[1 mark]*
$= 130.5407...$ cm
$= 131$ cm (to the nearest cm) *[1 mark]*

Section 6 — Probability and Statistics

Pages 63-64 — Probability

1 a) $\dfrac{2}{11}$ *[1 mark]*

b) $\dfrac{4}{11}$ *[1 mark]*

c) $\dfrac{2}{11}$ *[1 mark]*

2 $1 - \dfrac{1}{14} - \dfrac{1}{7} = \dfrac{14 - 1 - 2}{14} = \dfrac{11}{14}$ *[1 mark]*

3 a) $1 - \dfrac{3}{8} = \dfrac{5}{8}$ *[1 mark]*

b) $\dfrac{3}{8}$ *[1 mark]*

c) When there were 8 chocolates in the box, the probability of choosing a soft centre was $\dfrac{3}{8}$, so there were 3 chocolates with soft centres. After taking one, James is left with 7 chocolates in total, where only 2 have soft centres. The probability of choosing another is then $\dfrac{2}{7}$. *[1 mark]*

Section 6 — Probability and Statistics

Answers: P64 — P67

4 a)

	1	2	3	4	5	6
Head (H)	H1	H2	H3	H4	H5	H6
Tail (T)	T1	T2	T3	T4	T5	T6

[1 mark]

b) $\frac{1}{12}$ *[1 mark]*

c) $\frac{3}{12}$ or $\frac{1}{4}$ *[1 mark]*

5 a)

+	0	2	4	6	8	10
1	1	3	5	7	9	11
3	3	5	7	9	11	13
5	5	7	9	11	13	15
7	7	9	11	13	15	17

[2 marks available — 2 marks for all entries correct, otherwise 1 mark for at least 10 entries correct]

b) $\frac{3}{24}$ or $\frac{1}{8}$ *[1 mark]*

c) $\frac{10}{24}$ or $\frac{5}{12}$ *[1 mark]*

6 a) 7294, 7492, 7924, 7942 *[1 mark]*

b) 4 and 9 are square numbers.
3 out of 4 possibilities have either 4 or 9 as their second digit, so the probability is $\frac{3}{4}$. *[1 mark]*

Page 65 — Expected Frequency & Relative Frequency

1 a) $\frac{1}{5}$ *[1 mark]*

b) $\frac{1}{5} \times 500 = 100$ *[1 mark]*

2 E.g. The probability of a fair coin landing on heads is 0.5, so the coin should have landed on heads around 0.5 × 1000 = 500 times. *[1 mark]*
350 is a lot less than 500, so this coin does **not** appear to be fair. *[1 mark]*

You could also find relative frequency = 350 ÷ 1000 = 0.35. You'd expect an answer close to 0.5 for a fair coin.

3 a)

Number of rolls	Relative Frequency
1	19	0.16
2	23	0.19
3	21	0.18
4	17	0.14
5	21	0.18
6	19	0.16

[2 marks available — 2 marks for all correct, otherwise 1 mark for at least 4 correct]

b) The probability of landing on each number on a fair dice is $\frac{1}{6}$ = 0.1666... ≈ 0.17. So the relative frequency for each number on a fair dice should be around 0.17. *[1 mark]*
The relative frequencies for Olivia's dice are all quite close to 0.17 so yes, Olivia's dice seems to be fair. *[1 mark]*

c) The dice could be rolled a larger number of times. *[1 mark]*

Page 66 — Venn Diagrams

1 a) 6, 8, 10, 16 *[1 mark]*
b) 8, 10 *[1 mark]*
c) 6 *[1 mark]*
d) 5 *[1 mark]*

2 a) Number of customers who didn't choose either side dish = 50 − 18 − 7 − 12 = 13.

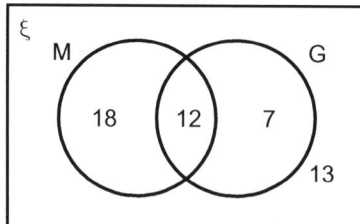

[2 marks available — 2 marks for diagram fully correct, otherwise 1 mark for 2 or 3 labels correct]

b) 18 + 7 + 12 + 13 = 50 customers in total
18 + 13 = 31 customers didn't want gravy
P(customer didn't want gravy) = $\frac{31}{50}$ *[1 mark]*

3 a) ξ = {1, 2, 3, 4, 5, 6, 7, 8, 9, 10, 11, 12, 13, 14, 15},
P = {1, 3, 5, 7, 9, 11, 13, 15} and Q = {3, 6, 9, 12, 15},
P ∩ Q = {3, 9, 15}

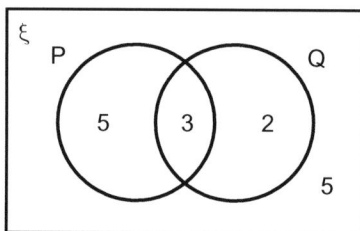

[3 marks available — 3 marks for completely correct diagram, otherwise award 1 mark for 2 numbers correct or 2 marks for 3 numbers correct]

b) 5 + 3 + 2 = 10 *[1 mark]*

c) 5 + 5 = 10 numbers are not multiples of 3, so P(not a multiple of 3) = $\frac{10}{15}$ or $\frac{2}{3}$ *[1 mark]*

Pages 67-68 — Graphs and Charts

1 a) Multiplier = 360 ÷ 45 = 8

Destination	Frequency	Angle of sector (°)
UK and Ireland	12	12 × 8 = 96°
Spain	15	15 × 8 = 120°
France	8	8 × 8 = 64°
USA	6	6 × 8 = 48°
Other	4	4 × 8 = 32°

[3 marks available — 3 marks for all correct, otherwise 1 mark for working out correct multiplier and 1 mark for at least 3 entries correct]

Section 6 — Probability and Statistics

Answers: P67— P69

b)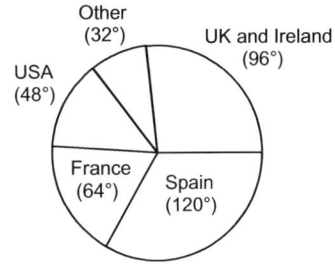

[2 marks available — 2 marks for completely correct diagram, otherwise 1 mark for correct angle in 3 or 4 sectors]

2 40° ÷ 20 = 2° per teenager
   360 ÷ 2 = 180 teenagers
   [2 marks available — 2 marks for correct answer, otherwise 1 mark for finding number of degrees per teenager]

3 a)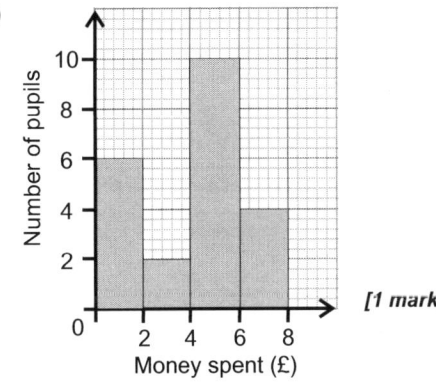
   [1 mark]

   b) 6 + 2 = 8 *[1 mark]*
   c) 6 + 2 + 10 + 4 = 22 *[1 mark]*

4 a)

Weight in kg (W)	Mid-Interval Value	Frequency
$0.5 \leq W < 1.0$	0.75	22
$1.0 \leq W < 1.5$	1.25	36
$1.5 \leq W < 2.0$	1.75	15
$2.0 \leq W < 2.5$	2.25	19
$2.5 \leq W < 3.0$	2.75	8

[1 mark]

b)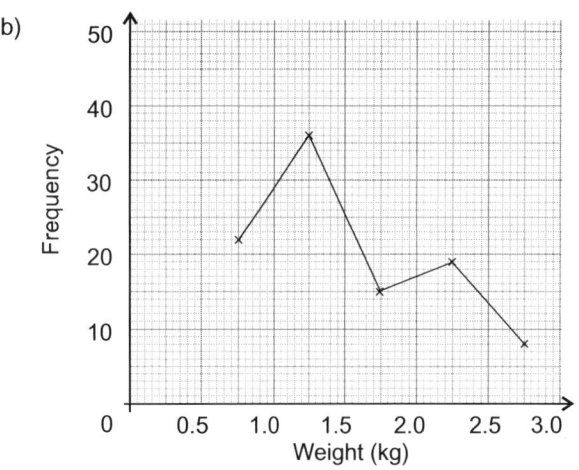

[2 marks available — 2 marks for all points correct and joined with straight lines, otherwise 1 mark for at least 3 points plotted correctly]

Page 69 — Mean, Median, Mode and Range

1 a) Numerical order:
      3, 3, 4, 5, 8, 9, 9, 9, 11, 12, 12, 15, 18, 20, 22
      $\frac{15 + 1}{2} = 8$, so the median is the 8th value.
      Median = 9 *[1 mark]*
   b) Mode = 9 *[1 mark]*
   c) Range = 22 − 3 = 19 *[1 mark]*

2 a) Discrete *[1 mark]*
   b) Mean = $\frac{26 + 12 + 4 + 4 + 4 + 7 + 11 + 16 + 18 + 5}{10}$ *[1 mark]*

      = £10.70 *[1 mark]*
   c) Numerical order:
      £4, £4, £4, £5, £7, £11, £12, £16, £18, £26
      There are 10 values, so the median is half way between the 5th and 6th numbers.
      Median = $\frac{7 + 11}{2}$ = £9 *[1 mark]*
   d) The 2 possibilities are 26 − 27 = -£1 and 4 + 27 = £31.
      He can't have spent a negative amount of money, so the answer is £31. *[1 mark]*

3 Let x be the third score:
   $\frac{25 + 32 + x}{3} = 30$ *[1 mark]*
   $\frac{25 + 32 + x}{3} \times 3 = 30 \times 3$
   25 + 32 + x = 90
   57 + x = 90
   57 + x − 57 = 90 − 57
   x = 33 *[1 mark]*

Section 6 — Probability and Statistics

Answers: P70 — P74

Page 70 — Averages from Frequency Tables

1. a)

Number of devices	Frequency	Number of devices × Frequency
1	55	55
2	68	136
3	75	225
4	25	100
5	15	75
6	8	48
7	4	28
TOTAL	250	667

[2 marks available — 2 marks for all entries correct, otherwise 1 mark for at least 4 entries correct]

b) 250 *[1 mark]*

c) $\frac{667}{250}$ = 2.668 *[1 mark]*

d) The number of devices with the highest frequency is 3, so the modal number is 3. *[1 mark]*

e) Total frequency = 250, so the median is half way between the 125th and 126th numbers.
125th = 3, 126th = 3, so the median = 3.
[2 marks available — 2 marks for correct answer, otherwise 1 mark for finding that the median is between the 125th and 126th numbers]

f) 7 − 1 = 6 *[1 mark]*

Page 71 — Averages from Grouped Frequency Tables

1. a)

Age in years	Frequency (f)	Mid-Interval Value (x)	f × x
15 to 19	125	17	2125
20 to 24	85	22	1870
25 to 29	40	27	1080
30 to 34	35	32	1120
35 to 39	15	37	555
TOTAL	300	—	6750

[2 marks available — 1 mark for each correct column]

b) 15 to 19 *[1 mark]*

c) 6750 ÷ 300 = 22.5 years *[1 mark]*

d) Total frequency = 300, so the median is half way between the 150th and 151st numbers.
150th is in "20 to 24", and 151st is in "20 to 24", so the median age group is "20 to 24".
[2 marks available — 2 marks for correct answer, otherwise 1 mark for finding that the median is between the 150th and 151st number]

2.

Time spent on internet (minutes)	Frequency	Mid-Interval Value (x)	f × x
0 ≤ time < 60	7	30	210
60 ≤ time < 120	12	90	1080
120 ≤ time < 180	22	150	3300
180 ≤ time < 240	9	210	1890
TOTAL	50	—	6480

$\frac{6480}{50}$ = 129.6 minutes

[3 marks available — 3 marks for correct answer, otherwise 1 mark for all mid-interval value entries correct and 1 mark for all f × x entries correct]

Page 72 — Scatter Graphs

1. a)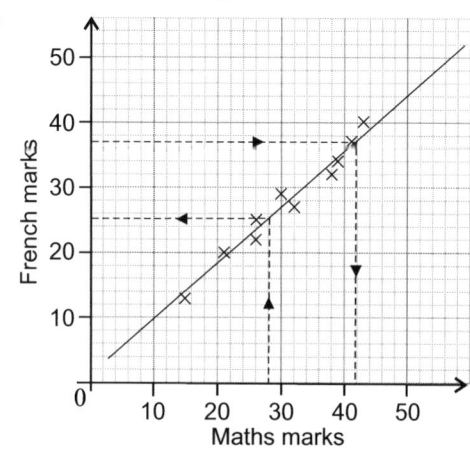

[2 marks available — 2 marks for all points correct, otherwise 1 mark for 5 or more points correct]

b) E.g. see diagram. *[1 mark]*

c) Strong positive correlation
[2 marks available — 2 marks for answer fully correct, otherwise 1 mark for 'positive']

d) 25 marks (accept 23-27) *[1 mark]*

e) 42 marks (accept 39-45) *[1 mark]*

Practice Paper 1 — Calculator NOT allowed

1. 17, 21 *[1 mark]*
The rule for the sequence is "add 4 to the previous number".
48, 96 *[1 mark]*
The rule for the sequence is "multiply the previous number by 2".

2. a) $\frac{15}{20} = \frac{75}{100}$ = 75% *[1 mark]*

   b) $\frac{12}{25} = \frac{48}{100}$ = 48% *[1 mark]*

3. $\frac{2}{5} = \frac{4}{10}$ = 0.4
35% = 0.35
0.25, 0.3, 35%, $\frac{2}{5}$

[2 marks available — 1 mark for converting each number into the same form, 1 mark for ordering them correctly]

Answers: P74 — P80

4   Exterior angle = 360° ÷ number of sides
So x = 360° ÷ 6 = 60°. *[1 mark]*
Interior angle = 180° − exterior angle
So y = 180° − 60° = 120°. *[1 mark]*

5 a) $3(5a + 2b) + 3b = 15a + 6b + 3b = 15a + 9b$ *[1 mark]*
  b) $(x + 3)(x − 4) = x^2 − 4x + 3x − 12$ *[1 mark]*
                     $= x^2 − x − 12$ *[1 mark]*

6 a) 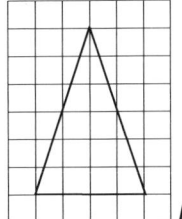
     [1 mark]
  b) 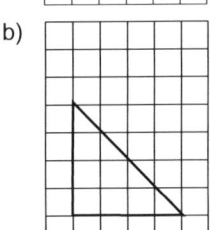 or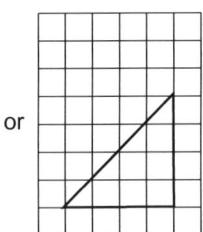
     [1 mark]

7   3 hours: £1.45 + 70p + 70p = £1.45 + 140p
= £1.45 + £1.40 = £2.85 *[1 mark]*
£5.00 − £2.85 = £2.15 *[1 mark]*

8 a) The marks are in increasing order, so the median is halfway between 7 and 8:
(7 + 8) ÷ 2 = 7.5 *[1 mark]*
  b) The range is 5 so the other mark is 10 − 5 = 5. *[1 mark]*
The other mark is NOT 8 + 5 = 13 as the test is only out of 10.

9 a) $2\frac{3}{4} + 3\frac{1}{2} = \frac{11}{4} + \frac{7}{2} = \frac{11}{4} + \frac{14}{4} = \frac{25}{4}$ km *[1 mark]*
  b) $7\frac{1}{4} - 3\frac{1}{2} = \frac{29}{4} - \frac{7}{2} = \frac{29}{4} - \frac{14}{4} = \frac{15}{4}$ km *[1 mark]*
  c) $\frac{25}{4} + \frac{15}{4} = \frac{40}{4} = 10$ km *[1 mark]*

10 a) (i) $\frac{1}{4} = \frac{5}{20}$, so it's **dark** chocolate. *[1 mark]*
     (ii) 20 − (12 + 5) = 3 biscuits are white chocolate.
So the probability is $\frac{3}{20}$. *[1 mark]*
  b) Chris eats 3 dark chocolate biscuits, so there are:
20 − 3 = 17 biscuits left and 12 are milk chocolate.
So the probability is $\frac{12}{17}$. *[1 mark]*
  c)

Type	Probability	Number of biscuits
Milk chocolate	$\frac{5}{8}$	(24 ÷ 8) × 5 = 3 × 5 = 15 *[1 mark]*
White chocolate	$\frac{3}{8}$	(24 ÷ 8) × 3 = 3 × 3 = 9 *[1 mark]*

11 a) $4x + 3 = x + 24$
$4x + 3 − 3 = x + 24 − 3$
$4x = x + 21$ *[1 mark]*
$4x − x = x + 21 − x$
$3x = 21$
$3x ÷ 3 = 21 ÷ 3$
$x = 7$ *[1 mark]*

  b) $2(5y + 8) = 6$
$10y + 16 = 6$ *[1 mark]*
$10y + 16 − 16 = 6 − 16$
$10y = -10$
$10y ÷ 10 = -10 ÷ 10$
$y = -1$ *[1 mark]*

12 a) The ratio of their ages is 4 : 6 so there are
4 + 6 = 10 parts.
One part will be £20 ÷ 10 = £2 *[1 mark]*
Six parts will be £2 × 6 = £12 *[1 mark]*
  b) In 5 years time Emma will be 9 years old and Steven will be 11 years old.
The ratio of their ages will be 9 : 11.
So there are 9 + 11 = 20 parts.
One part is £20 ÷ 20 = £1 *[1 mark]*
Nine parts are £1 × 9 = £9 *[1 mark]*

13 a)
[2 marks available — 1 mark for each 70° angle marked correctly]
∠PRQ is the other 70° angle in the isosceles triangle.
∠QRS is 70° because it is alternate to ∠PQR.
  b) ∠QRS = 70° so the other two angles in the isosceles triangle add to 180° − 70° = 110°. *[1 mark]*
The two missing angles are equal as the triangle is isosceles, so x = 110° ÷ 2 = 55°. *[1 mark]*

14 a) The pie chart represents 30 pupils.
So each pupil makes up 360° ÷ 30 = 12°.
Have a pet dog: 10 × 12° = 120°
Do not have a pet dog: 20 × 12° = 240°
[1 mark for giving both correct angles]
  b) Not possible to tell. *[1 mark]*
It could be that all 10 children with dogs also have a cat, or it could be that 15 of the 20 children without a dog have a cat instead. Or it could be anything in between.

15 a) In the first triangle the two missing angles are equal because the triangle's isosceles.
So both angles equal (180° − 30°) ÷ 2 = 75°.
In the second triangle one missing angle is 75° because the triangle's isosceles.
The other is 180° − 75° − 75° = 30°.
The triangles both have two 75° angles and one 30° angle so they are similar.
[2 marks available — 1 mark for finding the missing angles in each triangle, 1 mark for saying that triangles with the same angles are similar]
  b) No — the side opposite the 30° angle of each triangle is different. *[1 mark]*

16 a) True *[1 mark]*
Integers are just whole numbers (negative or positive).
  b) False *[1 mark]*
25 is a square number (5^2) but it is not a cube number.

17 a) $y = 0$ — line through D and C.
$x + y = 4$ — line through A and C.
$y = 2x + 4$ — line through A and B.
[2 marks available — 2 marks for joining all lines correctly, otherwise 1 mark for joining one line correctly]

Practice Paper 1

Answers: P80 — P86

b) Gradient = $\frac{0-(-4)}{4-(-4)} = \frac{4}{8} = \frac{1}{2}$
Line crosses y-axis at -2.
So the equation of the line is $y = \frac{1}{2}x - 2$ *[1 mark]*

18 a) $-6 < x \leq 6$ *[1 mark]*
b) 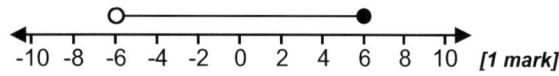 *[1 mark]*

19 a) A = {2, 3, 5, 7, 11}, B = {1, 2, 3, 4, 6, 8, 12},
A ∩ B = {2, 3}

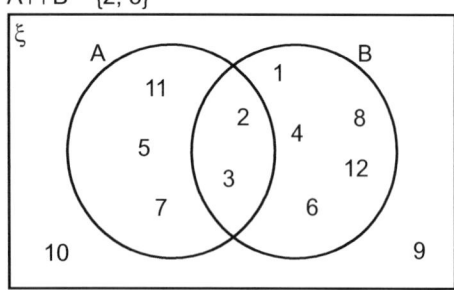

[2 marks available — 2 marks for putting all the numbers in the correct places on the diagram, otherwise 1 mark for a diagram with a maximum of 2 numbers in the wrong place]

b) A ∪ B = {1, 2, 3, 4, 5, 6, 7, 8, 11, 12}
So n(A ∪ B) = 10 *[1 mark]*

c) There are 3 elements that are prime and not a factor of 24 (5, 7 and 11). So the probability of picking one of these is:
$\frac{3}{12} = \frac{1}{4}$ *[1 mark]*
Prime and not a factor of 24 is the set A ∩ B'.

20 a)

Temperature (t °C)	Mid-interval value	Frequency
15 < t ≤ 20	(15 + 20) ÷ 2 = 17.5	1
20 < t ≤ 25	(20 + 25) ÷ 2 = 22.5	4
25 < t ≤ 30	(25 + 30) ÷ 2 = 27.5	6
30 < t ≤ 35	(30 + 35) ÷ 2 = 32.5	7
35 < t ≤ 40	(35 + 40) ÷ 2 = 37.5	2

[2 marks available — 1 mark for a completely correct mid-interval value column, 1 mark for a completely correct frequency column]

b) $30 < t \leq 35$ *[1 mark]*

c) Total frequency = 20, so the median is between the 10th and 11th values. *[1 mark]*
So the median is in the class $25 < t \leq 30$. *[1 mark]*

d)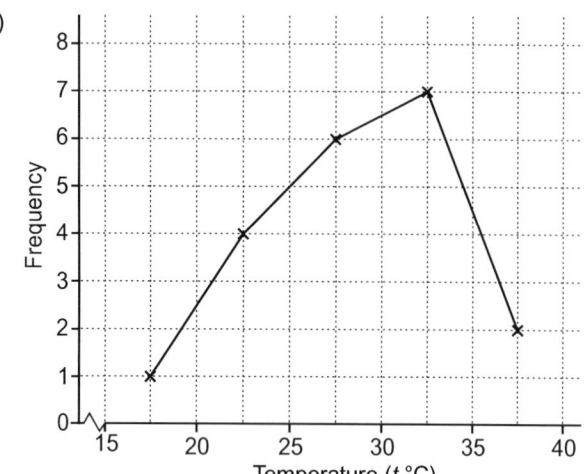

[2 marks available — 2 marks for a completely correct diagram, otherwise 1 mark for plotting at least 3 of the points correctly]

[There are 60 marks available in total for Paper 1]

Practice Paper 2 — Calculator allowed

1 a) 325 ÷13→ 25 −8→ 17 *[1 mark]*
b) 12 ×14→ 168 ÷8→ 21 *[1 mark]*

2 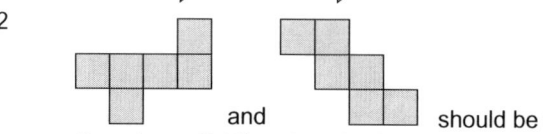 and should be ticked.

[2 marks available — 2 marks if only these two shapes are ticked, otherwise 1 mark if only one is ticked or 1 mark if an additional incorrect net is ticked]

3 a) 12 000 *[1 mark]*
b) 11 600 *[1 mark]*

4 a)

	Monthly Payment (£)	Total Repaid (£)
Bank A	179.94	6477.84
Bank B	193.38	193.38 × 36 = 6961.68
Bank C	189.35	189.35 × 36 = 6816.60

[2 marks available — 1 mark for the correct repayment for Bank B, 1 mark for the correct repayment for Bank C]

b) £6816.60 − £6477.84 = £338.76 *[1 mark]*

c) $\frac{£6477.84}{£5000} \times 100 = 129.5568\%$
= 129.6% (1 d.p.) *[1 mark]*

5 a) 6 × 2 × 4 = 48 cm³ *[1 mark]*
b) 4 × 3 × h = 48
12h = 48 *[1 mark]*
h = 4 cm *[1 mark]*

6 a) speed = 34 ÷ 3 = 11.3333... km/h
= 11.3 km/h (1 d.p.) *[1 mark]*
b) distance = 4 × 12.3 = 49.2 km *[1 mark]*
90 km − 49.2 km − 34 km = 6.8 km *[1 mark]*

Practice Paper 2

Answers: P86 — P90

7 a)
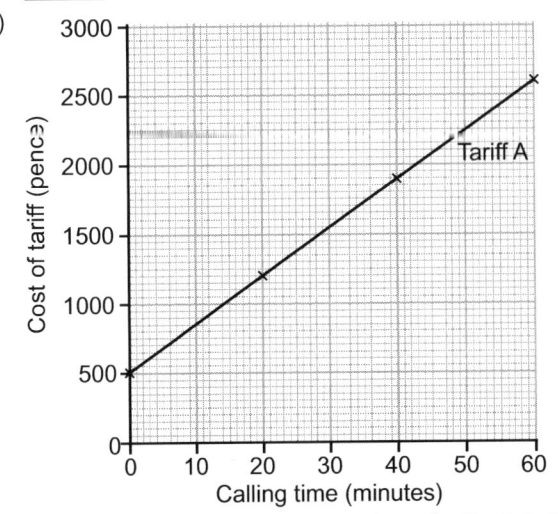
(factor tree: 399 → 21, 19; 21 → 3, 7)   *[1 mark]*

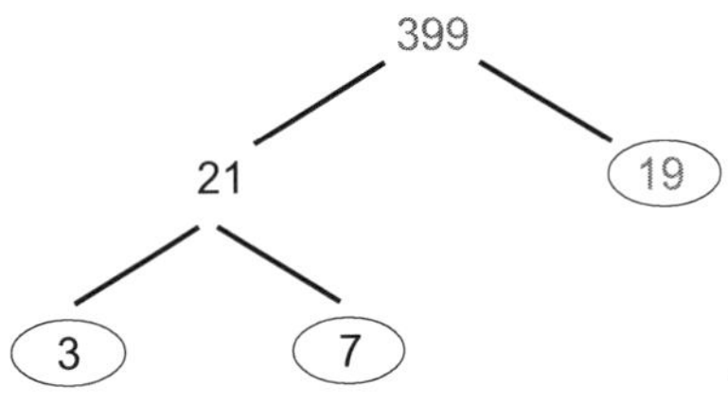

b) 3 × 7 × 19 *[1 mark]*

8 a) 56 cm × π = 175.92918... cm
= 176 cm to the nearest cm *[1 mark]*

b) 142 × 175.92918... cm = 24981.9447... cm
= 249.819447... m = 250 m (to the nearest m) *[1 mark]*

9 a) 1 g provides 40.5 ÷ 150 = 0.27 g
200 g provides 0.27 g × 200 = 54 g *[1 mark]*

b) 100 g of tuna provides:
(171 kcal ÷ 150) × 100 = 114 kcal
100 g of salmon provides 255 kcal ÷ 2 = 127.5 kcal
So 100 g of salmon contains more energy.
[2 marks available — 2 marks for working out the amount of energy in tuna and salmon and giving the correct answer, otherwise 1 mark for working out the amount of energy in either tuna or salmon correctly]

10 a) P(French) = P(Russian) × 3
= 0.1 × 3 = 0.3 *[1 mark]*
P(German) = 1 – 0.3 – 0.35 – 0.1 = 0.25 *[1 mark]*

b) Number of students expected to choose Spanish:
0.35 × 240 = 84
Number of students expected to choose Russian:
0.1 × 240 = 24
84 – 24 = 60
So you would expect 60 more pupils to take Spanish than Russian.
[2 marks available — 1 mark for finding the number of students choosing one language, 1 mark for finding the number of students choosing the other language and finding the difference]

11 a) For 20 minutes it costs 500 + (20 × 35) = 1200p.
For 60 minutes it costs 500 + (60 × 35) = 2600p.

Calling time (minutes)	0	20	40	60
Cost of tariff (pence)	500	1200	1900	2600

[1 mark]

b)
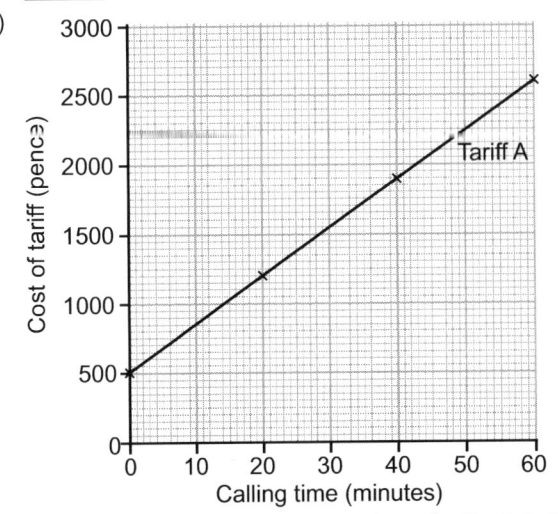

[1 mark for a straight line passing through all points from the table]

c) For 0 minutes it costs 0p.
For 50 minutes it costs (50 × 48) = 2400.

Calling time (minutes)	0	25	50
Cost of tariff (pence)	0	1200	2400

[1 mark]

d)
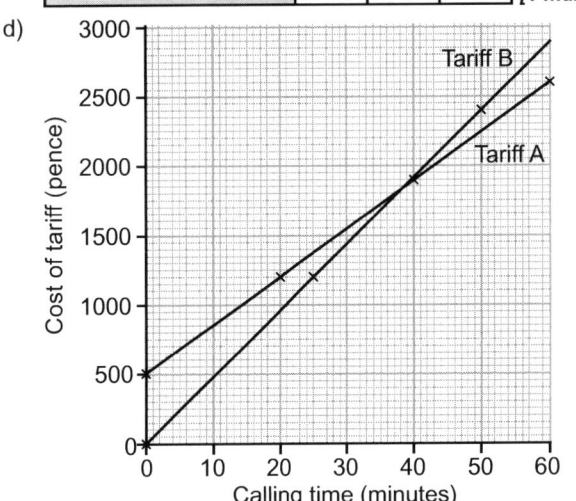

[1 mark for a straight line passing through all points from the table]

e) 38 minutes *[1 mark — allow 37, 38 or 39 minutes]*
Find the x-coordinate where the lines cross.

12 a) 800 000 000 = 8 × 10⁸ *[1 mark]*

b) 1.2 × 10⁻⁴ = 0.00012 *[1 mark]*

c) 800 000 000 × (1.2 × 10⁻⁴) = 8 × 10⁸ × 1.2 × 10⁻⁴
= 8 × 1.2 × 10⁸⁻⁴
= 9.6 × 10⁴ *[1 mark]*

13 a) C = 13n + 51 *[1 mark]*

b) 129 = 13n + 51 *[1 mark]*
78 = 13n
6 = n
So she hires the skip for 6 days. *[1 mark]*

14 a) Call the length of the shortcut x, then:
x² = 23² + 14² = 725
x = √725 = 26.9258... m
= 27 m (to the nearest m) *[1 mark]*

b) 23 m + 14 m – 26.9258... m = 10.0741... m
= 10 m (to the nearest m) *[1 mark]*

15
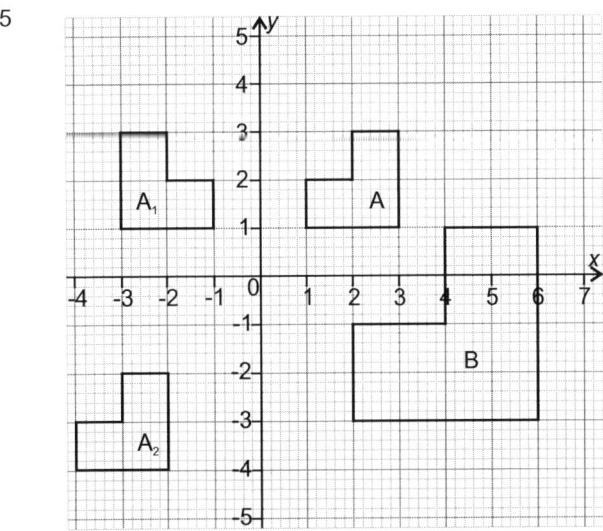

a) *[1 mark for correctly drawing and labelling shape A₁]*
b) *[1 mark for correctly drawing and labelling shape A₂]*

Practice Paper 2

Answers: P90 — P92

c) Translation ***[1 mark]*** by the vector $\begin{pmatrix} -5 \\ -5 \end{pmatrix}$ ***[1 mark]***

<u>OR</u> Reflection ***[1 mark]*** in the line $y = -x - 1$. ***[1 mark]***

d) Enlargement by scale factor 2 ***[1 mark]*** with centre of enlargement (0, 5). ***[1 mark]***

16 a) (0, -3) ***[1 mark]***

b) $x = -2.8$ ***[1 mark]*** and $x = 1.8$ ***[1 mark]***

Draw the line y = 2 and find the x-coordinates where it intersects the curve.

17 a) $\frac{9\text{ cm}}{6\text{ cm}} = 1.5$ ***[1 mark]***

So the lengths in PQR are 1.5 times as long as those in ABC.

PR = 10 cm × 1.5 = 15 cm ***[1 mark]***

b) BC = 16.5 ÷ 1.5 = 11 cm ***[1 mark]***

c) AB : PQ = 6 : 9 = 2 : 3 ***[1 mark]***

18 a) Stoneholt is 10 cm ***[1 mark]*** away from Goldmill which corresponds to 10 × 2 = 20 km. ***[1 mark]***

b)

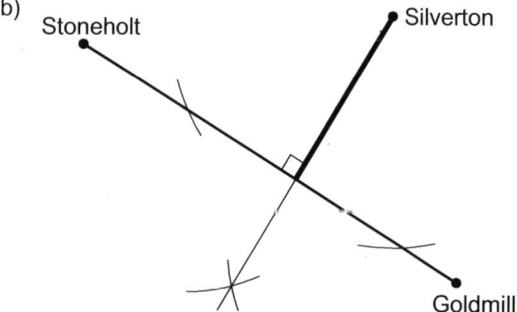

[2 marks available — 1 mark for correctly drawn construction lines, 1 mark for drawing the path correctly]

19 Call the length of the sloping side of the ramp x.

$\sin 10° = \frac{70}{x}$ ***[1 mark]***

$x = \frac{70}{\sin 10°} = 403.1139...\text{ cm}$ ***[1 mark]***

$= 4.031139...\text{ m}$

$= 4.03\text{ m}$ (to the nearest cm) ***[1 mark]***

[There are 60 marks available in total for Paper 2]

ISBN 978 1 78294 175 0
9 781782 941750
MHQA32
£2.00
(Retail Price)
www.cgpbooks.co.uk